AF668167

GHOND THE HUNTER

GHOND THE HUNTER

DHAN GOPAL MUKERJI

MANOHAR
2025

First published 1900
Reprinted 2024, 2025

© Manohar Publishers & Distributors, 2024

All rights reserved. No part of this publication may be reproduced or transmitted, in any form or by any means, without prior permission of the author and the publisher.

ISBN 978-81-19139-57-6

Published by
Ajay Kumar Jain *for*
Manohar Publishers & Distributors
4753/23 Ansari Road, Daryaganj
New Delhi 110 002

Printed at
Replika Press Pvt. Ltd.

GHOND THE HUNTER

BY

DHAN GOPAL MUKERJI

ILLUSTRATED BY

BORIS ARTZYBASHEFF

LONDON & TORONTO

J. M. DENT & SONS, LTD.

TO THE MEMORY OF

PRADHAN THE SANTAL

THE ORIGINAL OF GHOND

CONTENTS

ILLUSTRATIONS

GHOND THE HUNTER

I—First Adventure with a Poisonous Snake

FROM America comes your letter commanding me to dictate to the village scribe the adventures that befell me from childhood on. You say in your epistle that if the history of my life is recorded it will give pleasure and joy to children of that far-off America where houses are reared so high that they touch the stars. I wish I could tell of anything very tall. But a poor hunter whose knowledge of books is very small has to satisfy himself with dwarfish events that clutter up the pavement of his existence.

Since I write rarely, if at all, I have sent for the scribe of our village. He tells me that he will charge me less per page since what I have to dictate is not going to be a love letter. You know very well, O boy of my training, scribes charge more for love letters because they have to be richly ornamented with numerous adjectives. And adjectives cost money.

Though I do not have to write my adventures down, I have to relate them. No easy task that for a man whose speech is the dialect of the peasantry, destitute of elegance and half bare like the ill-clad bodies of those who till the earth in India. Like the Hindu husbandman's, my mind too is empty of all things. Nay, worse still, it is but a nest of errors.

Yet, O Beloved of Felicity, I shall display before you the years of my training in the Indian jungles where beasts and birds grow with the same abundance as fancies under a lunatic's skull. There is no telling whence they come and what purpose they fulfill. But while they live, their ways are as definite as men's, and their sense of good behaviour if not nobler is at least as orderly as if they dwelt in houses and drove in horse-pulled cars.

Since a tale must have a beginning as the thread in the cotton in the spinner's hand, let me speak first of my family and home.

I was born almost an orphan. Save for an old aunt who nurtured me in my infancy, I had no one to call my own. I am told that both of my parents died in an epidemic of typhoid when I was a few months old. Then it was that my father's old widowed sister, Kuri, adopted me. She brought me up in my father's house in the village of Mayavati.

My earliest recollection of our village and home turns on an unpleasant incident. We had gone to a meeting of the community late one afternoon to consider some problems that had been troubling the village. Whenever there took place a crime, a quarrel, or an untoward event, the village Panchayat, the meeting of Pancha, five, ayat, old representatives, was called to deliberate and recommend action about it.* That particular afternoon some crime had to be talked over, so the representatives of the village were asked to meet. My Kuri, because she was one of the oldest citizens and also the head of our household, was entitled to a seat in the Council of the Panchayat. And that afternoon since all the servants were away and she could not leave me at home alone, she took me with her. At the time I was a little over five years old.

The meeting was held on the Communal threshing floor. Every village in India has a common threshing floor where the grain of the community is threshed during harvest time. It is considered more or less sacred, for here the grain is separated from the chaff, and food, Mother earth's gift of consecration, is found by men and women, her eldest born. The floor consists of a vast slab of stone about ten feet in diameter. In its centre there is a long deep hole.

* Pancha—Anglo-Saxon Folk moot. Hindu council of five.

There in harvest time a bamboo pole, green as a parrot, is driven. To it then is attached a long, smooth bamboo bar about six feet long which serves as a yoke. Then two or three oxen are yoked under it. After all has been made ready the new-mown harvest is strewn on the floor and the oxen are driven round and round, separating by their tread the rice and wheat from the stalk. Later on they separate in the same way the kernel from the chaff. When the beasts of burden are not working, human beings do their threshing with the old fashioned flails instead.

To return to our story. The afternoon that I had mentioned was in the spring. The threshing floor had not been used all winter. The hole in the centre held no bamboo pole in it and it lay, as we sat closely around it, gaping at us like the sinister eye of a blind monster.

Since the sunset was at hand, our village priest, Purohit, opened the meeting with the old prayer:

> "May understanding permeate our efforts,
> May we never quarrel
> May God enjoy us."

after which a short meditation followed. I, who was too young to meditate, looked at the faces of the half a dozen old people around me. With the exception of my aunt, Kuri, all of them were men, and all very old and sedate. But she, the head of our household, though older even than the men, appeared younger and stronger. Now I looked above at the bough of the sacred Banyan tree under which we sat. One massive limb spread its branches over us like a canopy; the light of the sunset ran along it in vermilion veins. Far off a turtle-dove cooed and swifts flew cheeping in the sky. Herons flew far above them going north, a tangible thread across the intangible blue. I wondered how high they were—two times a mountain or three? Again, drawn by what curiosity I know not, I lowered my eyes to scan the faces of the human beings about me but perceiving that their meditation was over, I removed my glance and fixed it on the hole in the threshing floor. Presently I felt as though something were moving there. Like black water something was brimming over. In an instant I recognised it—a cobra's head! I shouted: "Snake, snake!" The assembly, which had just finished its meditation, was taken by such a shock of surprise that most of them, ere they knew what they were doing, jumped and ran. Few realised that it is dangerous to run from a frightened, poisonous snake. He had already raised his head and was swaying from side to side, while his tongue licked the air rapidly. He was very near me. My aunt, who had seen all in a glance, and the old priest, were the only two of the committee who had not run away. "Sit still like a stone," commanded my aunt. That was not easy for a boy of five, but I did my best.

You know why one should not move before a snake. His eyes are set where men's ears are placed —at the sides of his head, and he cannot focus them as we focus our eyes. If a snake raises his head he can see a thing when it moves, so when you face an angry snake, the best thing to do is to keep still. I did so. But a beast that is frightened does not recover himself quickly. The viper before me was no exception. He kept swaying from side to side and flicking his tongue in the air like the end of a lash. In the meantime day was passing into night; it was growing darker every moment.

The priest said to my aunt: "My cane is two feet behind me. If I get it I can smite him. Very slowly I shall walk backwards toward it, but do you remain still as tombstones the while."

I could hear him move as softly as a man taking off a tunic from his body. But just as he had reached and grasped his stick, the snake leaped like black lightning and buried its fangs in Kuri's foot. I shrieked in terror, while the priest hit the horrible fellow again and again with his stick. At last he killed it. My aunt who had been standing steady suddenly sat down as if she were dying. The priest tore open his tunic and brought out a knife. Swiftly he cut off the small toe, the end of which the snake had bitten. Blood began to flow freely. He then put his mouth to the wounded spot and sucked out a mouthful of blood and spat it out. I had never seen such presence of mind as that priest's. He proceeded to tear off quite a little of his tunic and bandage Kuri's foot with it. By now the whole village had joined us with lanterns, staves and pitchforks. The gods alone knew what they wanted to do with pitchforks!

That night we put my aunt to bed in our house after her wound had been cauterized by the village doctor. The next day she had a slight fever, that was all. Had it not been for the priest's resourcefulness she would have been dead in a few hours.

After that adventure of ours the priest began to take an interest in me. He became my first teacher, and without him I would not know half the secrets of the jungle.

II—The Village Festival

WHEN I was about eight years old, I began to notice things as a whole. Hitherto the events of the day, such as morning prayers and evening silence, had seemed islands of peace in a chaos of meaningless unrelated events, and people went to work, came home from the fields, went to bed, and each one of these actions appeared an invention of the moment. It never occurred to my child's mind that they formed the parts of a whole and were not mere unrelated incidents.

But a little before my eighth birthday a change was wrought in my perceptions when one of our cows gave birth to a heifer. I was entrusted with the task of looking after the calf when she was weaned from her mother six weeks later. "The cowbell before the cow" is a proverb of the hills, and so my first care was to go to the smith for a brass bell. After that I had to call on the weaver for a cotton string which would be thick but soft enough for the tender young neck of Goma, which was the name I gave my little charge. Whenever she mooed it sounded Go-Ma, meaning "O my mother, where art thou?" In the course of a fortnight I learned that the weaver, the blacksmith, the vendor of hay, were all related to me and my little cow.

One more experience revealed to my poor little mind the unity of life. It occurred during the Dipavali festival—the feast of lanterns—which as you know, is held after the autumn rain is over, and is a kind of thanksgiving and harvest-home celebration. During that day in late October all the cows of our village were led in procession through its chief thoroughfare to the communal threshing floor, there to be let loose to wander home all by themselves.

My aunt and myself owned the third largest flock of cattle in the village, consisting of twenty cows, so ours had the third place in the procession. But no farmer displays all his cows; he generally selects half a dozen fine heads of cattle. I was charged with choosing our six finest beasts to walk in the procession. First of all I took Goma, then her mother, three more cows and our bull Vrisa.

The selection was made in the morning. The rest of the day I spent with one of our farm hands in washing and decorating the beasts. We took them to the river which ran at the south end of the village. The village ran from east to west and to our north bristled the Himalayas. After their bath the animals were brought home to be decorated. First of all we painted each adult animal's horns in yellow. Then we strung garlands of red oleanders around their necks, and over their backs we flung purple, blue, orange, green and silver shawls which were securely tied by strings round their glistening rumps. Next we painted their hoofs yellow. It took nearly the whole day before my flock was ready to march in the procession. Goma, who had not yet grown horns, nor a back ample enough to be covered with a gem-shaming shawl, had to walk with nothing on but her brass bell. At the eleventh hour someone suggested that we should paint her hoofs yellow like the others, but I protested: "She shall wear no gold on her feet until she has horns to paint like shining banana skins. Not till then!"

My aunt, who agreed with me, ordered us to march along to the village temple whence the procession was to start. Our bull, Vrisa, garlanded in red oleander, his horns gleaming like spikes of gold, his back a shimmer of emerald, while his dewlap peeped out like shining steel in between clusters of flaming flowers, led our flock. Next to him marched our chief cowherd clad in spotless white and turbaned in tawny silk. He held a green bamboo stave in his left hand while his right rested on Vrisa's mountainous rump that swayed from side to side like the head of a sleepy child. I led the rear with Goma whose tinkling bell fretted the silence of the early evening.

Our house was the last one at the northern end of the village, and we were obliged to go far to the west to reach the temple compound, for the house of Heaven, as we called our village shrine, lay at the western end so that at dawn the rising sun's light fell on it in its purest splendour. It was a miracle of yellow sandstone about three storeys high. In front of it spread a lawn large enough to accommodate more than five hundred people. Behind the shrine, out of sight, lay the low one-storeyed house of the priest.

Slowly our Vrisa, throbbing with colours and fat, walked on to the green lawn, and stood facing the shrine. Soon from different directions came pouring flocks of cattle, their horns all yellow flame and their flanks dripping with stabbing colours. In no time the place was filled with the noise of men and beasts. Now the priest appeared on the top of the temple steps to give his benediction. He was robed in ochre. Slowly he lifted his hands and blessed us:

Eka avarno Bahudha
Shakti
Yogat

He the Infinite Compassion
Untainted by colour, unfettered by form,
He, who satisfies the need of all races and all forms of Life.

He, to whom all colours are as inviolate as all souls,
He has satisfied your longings at the beginning, as well as at the ending of all the worlds.
Peace be unto you
Beast and men, may you live in peace,
May you bring peace to all!

Just as the priest had finished, my little charge ran forward tinkling her bell. This was in good taste, I thought, for it marked the end of the ceremony at the temple. Now the procession formed itself, and we started for the communal threshing floor at the eastern extremity of our village. Shall I ever forget the wonder of that march?

We passed between houses some of adobe with thatched roofs, some of brick and timber—but all filled that afternoon with faces of men and women not only of our village but from the neighbouring city of Almora who had come to witness our festival. The hitherto dusty road that traversed our village had been swept and strewn with grains of rice, lotus leaves, and drawings and designs had been made by different families on their front walls and also in the dust of their thresholds. From every house rose a trumpeting sound of conch-shells blown by women, and over our heads were strewn flowers by young girls. One could hardly see the ruddy evening sky above our heads because of the Bel-leaves (cedar leaves) and little flowers that swarmed in the air ere they fell upon us.

At last we reached the communal threshing floor under the vast banyan tree where the village elders and my aunt Kuri received us. Here the elders blessed us before dismissing the cortège. The oldest one said: "We are all brothers—man and beast. We are sharers in toil and suffering pain. We partake of one another's well-being: the life that is in the ox is the same life that beats in our blood: the milk that comes from the cow is the strength that is in our children's limbs. May you treat your animals well; may they in turn be moved by God to serve you abundantly."

With these words the gathering was dismissed. Just then Goma, that little mischief-maker, walked forward and began to devour the oleander garland from the neck of the bull at the head of the procession. This was both terrible and humiliating in spite of the fact that she was hungry and only two months old. Had the owner of the bull been a good man he would have understood and forgiven, but instead he rushed forward in a rage and began to beat her back. Instantly she switched her tail, twisted her neck and frisked off in the direction of the jungle and I followed after! It did not take us long to be out of the reach of the men and women at the threshing floor. I saw nothing but Goma's vanishing white body before me. I stumbled, fell, rose and ran again after her. Before she had stopped running and before I knew where we were, it had grown quite dark.

Both of us suddenly realised that we had penetrated the outskirts of the jungle and were at the threshold of great danger. To ordinary observers the outer edges of a forest may seem safe at all times, but to those who know, evening and early morning are the two occasions when it is not safe to be there. At those times animals are going out to hunt or returning from their night's outing. Any man who lingers on the outskirts of a dense jungle may be killed by a tiger or leopard; a boy and a calf are in greater danger, because wild dogs, wolves, hyenas, and black panthers all seek to devour them.

So there we stood wondering about our fate in that Dipavali evening. In a moment there flashed through my mind the pictures of previous nights at Dipavali when the whole village was illuminated with lights, every house decorating its roof and walls with innumerable lamps. The village put on magic for a dress. But now behold, here I was lost in the jungle in the company of a cow hardly two months old!

Fortunately Goma had not yet learned to be afraid. Fear is taught by grown up men and beasts to their young. Once we learn to be afraid, we rarely shake off the habit, and I believe our fear frightens other beasts causing them to attack us. While Goma stood there looking at me between eating mouthfuls of leaves from the surrounding dense saplings, I thought how hard it would be to find a way out in the surrounding dark, eloquent with a thousand noises of insects and animals. These sounds, however, betokened comparative safety, for were a tiger moving in our direction, all voices would have been hushed. "The more noise the safer the jungle" runs the proverb.

I put my hand on Goma's shoulder and started to lead her back. We kept steadily to the windward of the noises, but we had to do a good deal of tacking to avoid the less noisy places. After we had gone about half an hour, we were able to discern through the surrounding wall of foliage what I thought to be a haze of light in the sky betokening our nearness to the town of Mayavati. I felt happy, and Goma switched her tail in pleasure. But danger swoops down on you when you relax your vigilance. Something fell at our feet crushing under it all the insect and other noises that were running like water in the undergrowth. Goma groaned, then leaped. In a moment she was out of touch or hearing. I stood still, wondering at the heavy thing lying on the floor of the jungle. I kept on walking backwards and peering into the midnight dark before me. Nothing could I see, but I heard shush—sha—shush near me. It kept on drawing nearer and nearer. I was convinced that it must be a python. If there had been a strong tree near by I would have been lost, for the snake with its tail around the trunk for a lever could have held me so firmly in its coil that escape would have been impossible. But fortunately we were passing through grassy fields interspersed with saplings hardly ten feet high, too frail for the great snake to coil around. The moment I realised the nature of my enemy, I turned on my heels and ran, knowing that he could not catch me if I ran zig-zagging away from him. I had not gone very far when I met a search party from the village out with lanthorns and spikes looking for me. I was indeed very glad to see them. They had been searching for Goma and myself for nearly an hour. On my arrival home we found the calf already there. She had dashed from the jungle straight to the cowshed.

When I told the men who found me and my aunt about my having encountered a python they would hardly believe me, saying: "This is the tale of a frightened child." I was deeply chagrined but alas, they did not know that in another week's time they would pay for the folly of their scepticism.

III—The Python Works Its Havoc

I MUST give you some further description of our village before our story travels any further. How can I tell of the ways of parrots if I do not first describe the forest in which they live?

As well as at the communal threshing floor and the temple grounds, people met and talked with one another by the river Avati, which was about the twentieth of a mile broad and too shallow for navigation, though during the spring when the snows melted in the Himalayas, or the rains swelled its waters in July, Avati attained the depth of nearly a dozen feet for a fortnight at a time. But the current was so swift at that season that swimming or floating on it meant utter disaster. The river ran between banks of ilex, deodar and plane trees, and here and there its northern shore was pierced and secured by stone walls and yellow sandstone stairways commonly known as Ghauts. During the rainy season Avati would turn as tawny as the steps themselves but at other times she was as clear and bright as the eyes of a bird.

There on the Ghauts people met when they came to fetch water, about nine in the morning, an hour before bathing began. Since it was a one way current, without tides, whatever water was muddied after the drinking water was taken, became clear for the bathers downstream, and whatever they sullied, flowed out eastwards to the sea. The water was always clean. In the afternoon people bathed in it again before going to the temple for evening meditation, and about midday between the times when men made use of it, the animals bathed in Avati, and drank from it whenever they chose. We always took our cattle there at half past eleven and gave them their bath. It was wonderful to see their red, white and grey sides drawn into the silver water, in whose depths the tall trees of the bank flung their reflections like torches of green.

One late November morning when women had come to fetch water from the river, they saw a python floating down stream. They came home and told their men-folk, but those of us who were in the fields did not hear of it, and punctually at eleven thirty we brought our herds of cattle to give them their bath. With the help of one of our hired men, I was busy scrubbing my beasts with straw as they came out of the water usually one by one, but when two came out together, the hired man took one and I the other. After they had been rubbed, they were sent down for a final dip. When they came out at last their sleek sides would drip with lambent water in the midday sun.

It was when Goma and her mother had come up from the stream and the hired man and I had begun to rub them—I of course taking Goma—that suddenly a black rope swung down from a tree above and gathered the cow, and then my poor man in its swift circling coil. In a trice, where stood the two of them, groaned a dying man amid the bellows of a dying beast. Goma and the rest of the herd fled in panic leaving me face to face with the horrible spectacle. I will never forget how the few feet of that serpent's tail thinned itself almost to the size of a child's wrist as it hung from the tree, tightening as its body stretched and then letting go as the coils dropped upon its victims. Ere he and the poor cow became crushed into pulp I fled from the spot.

It was not long before I met herds of cattle running pell-mell through the village streets. Apparently our stampeding herd had run into other people's cattle coming down to the river for their bath, and had communicated to them their panic. I shouted to the herdsmen the news of the calamity that I had witnessed on the river bank. Call after call was sounded by the priest at his temple on his conch shell.

Alas, by the time the village rallied to the river they found neither python nor victims. None knew where to search. But I told Kuri I was sure the monster could be found very near the place of the tragedy. So when in the evening we went to the temple to hear the priest read the scriptures and the epics, we drew him into a corner and I unburdened my mind to him. The grey-beard listened to me carefully, and said: "Take me tomorrow morning. I must now take my seat at the altar and read to you the story of Rama."

Later on, I shall tell you of those readings that our priest gave in the temple every evening, and of the morality plays that were acted there at least once a month.

The following day after I had brought flowers to the temple and prayed there, the priest and I set out to find the murderer. I took him first to the outer jungle where I had encountered the enemy during the Dipavali evening. It proved an easy task in daylight. Lo, there lay long lines of grass and dry leaves crushed in a certain pattern. We followed it wherever it led. Those long sweeping lines thick as my waist could only have been made by a python. It did not take us long to reach the river bank. No doubt he had gone there to take a drink. And while he was at it something from behind had frightened him and he fell into the swift current. The latter had borne him down past the Ghaut where human beings bathed. At last he reached the place where the river takes a sharp turn and where we always bathed the cattle. There the current is retarded by a kind of dam made by fallen boulders. We traced him as far as the soft ground on which he had crawled and the tree around which he had coiled his muddy body. After that we faced a perfect blank.

Purohit, the priest, and I tried hard to locate his

present whereabouts but in vain. Dejected in spirit and baffled in mind, we sat down on the shore about midday just to rest our tired limbs. Slowly herdsmen brought their herds and bathed them. One by one the cows and oxen went home. At last came our own herd led by a new hired man named Gokul. He plunged into the water ahead of his charge. Then followed little Goma just to show that she too could share Gokul's fun. They played with each other in the water like children. It amused me so to see my little heifer so frisky and happy. I called her name. She obeyed instantly. She started toward the shore. Slowly, inch by inch, she struggled up. When she was ready to put her feet on dry ground, her eyes fell on something to her left. Then she stopped. As if she had seen death itself, her body quivered in terror. That was enough for the keen eye of the priest. He dashed forward into the water and stood waist deep looking at the spot where the calf's eyes were riveted. He shouted with joy: "Mila, Mila!" (Found! Found!) That noise dug into Goma's being like a goad. She was driven up the shore by that "Mila, Mila," and ran home. The other cattle followed her example. The drumming of their hoofs on the ground frightened the python apparently, for the priest called to me to look before he also ran away.

The python could not creep away nor fight. He had eaten too much. It would take him at least a month to digest a youth of twenty and a medium-sized cow. I went into the water and stood near the priest. I looked and looked. At last under a tree from which the river, after eating half the ground, had receded, I saw something. Two eyes like dull crystals, and below them two protruding brown things like tusses. He looked like a most sinister image of Satan lying under the outer roots of a maple and the thick shadows cast by its bough that overhung many feet of water. A black mountain of half coiled python looking at us with glassy eyes and out of the corner of its mouth protruding the two horns of our cow! The uncanny sight filled me with loathing and terror. It takes a serpent a long time to dissolve the horns of its victim in its own saliva. As you know, snakes large or small, cannot chew; they partly crush their food in their throats. The priest said: "Let us catch him alive."

We went to the village which had heard of the python's presence from our new herdsman, Gokul. The able-bodied men asked advice of the serpent charmers who said the snake was too large to be caught by the flute, so the men set to work to erect a cage of bamboo and cowhide thongs which took a day to finish. When it was done it was lowered in front of the python. But now the problem was to get him to move into it. Noises, shouts, then men jumping over the roots of the tree, all failed to make him move an inch. There he lay, gripped by the act of digesting his food, a process more powerful than himself. The open cage was pushed close enough to the cavern mouth under the tree to allow just room enough for the front door, which was held up by a rope to the overhanging branch, to fall guillotine fashion, once he was inside.

But he did not budge from his place. So all the people left in disgust, saying: "What a stupid snake."

It was about the fourth day after our finding his hiding place that I went alone to carry out a plan of my own. When I reached the spot there was no adult about. I fetched pick, shovel, straw and a lot of kindling wood. Next I dug a tunnel at the python's back, which was a slanting hole, descending deeper and deeper as it approached the beast. As I was half way through Purohit appeared. When he saw me he approved of my plan, and threw aside his priest's beads and cudgel, and took the pick from my already tired hands. He kept on digging harder and harder, and after we had worked another two hours, at about four in the afternoon he said: "I can hear him breathe. Go and get a crowbar."

When I fetched it he took it and jammed it right through the thin partition of loose soil and struck the serpent. He moved. We heard the roots of the tree tremble as his heavy body fell against them. But he did not move enough to please the priest. He jabbed a few times more, without getting a satisfactory result from the sleepy monster.

Then we laid the straw thick in the tunnel, almost next to the python's skin, then covered it with dry autumn leaves. After placing the kindling wood on top, we set the tunnel on fire. I was ordered to go up the tree with a knife. I climbed away over and lay on the overhanging branch to which was tied the rope, that held up the door of the prison prepared for our enemy. My orders were to cut the rope as soon as the snake had entered the cage.

Slowly the smoke arose, and as luck would have it, lay in thick layers between me and everything below. In time it rose higher and began to hurt my eyes. I shouted to the priest a warning: "Call to me as loud as you can when the python enters the cage and you want the door to snap down, for I can see nothing. When I hear you I shall cut the rope."

Purohit shouted: "If he gets into the cage I will shout so that it will make you deaf. As soon as you hear me, cut that rope."

Whirl upon whirl of smoke arose, choking my nostrils and blinding my eyes. There I sat with my face over that all-powerful incense fume. I shut my eyes and concentrated all attention to catching the priest's warning cry. Of course the more I listened the more I heard the hiss and crackle of the fire and the noise of human voices. Apparently the whole village had repaired there to witness the roasting of the python. They kept on talking to one another and sometimes shouting aloud. How on earth I could complete my task under those circumstances passed my comprehension.

It seemed as if hours passed. I was like one wrapped in midnight darkness of smoke and noise. Suddenly a dizzy spell seized me. I felt as if I should fall off the tree. I heard an awful uproar. In the midst of the thunderous racket I faintly heard someone say in a squeaking voice: "O thou grandsire of a monkey, cut the rope. Dost thou not hear me, O half brother of a mule? Cut that rope."

But he who was abusing me did not know that I could see nothing in the smoke. All the same I blindly groped forward and slashed away under the bough with my knife, mostly cutting the air. But I persisted. Once I cut off a twig. Another time I thought I cut a branch. Then another branch—no, this was no branch! Ha, the rope! I went on sawing away at it. Harder and harder I worked. And by the increasing din and tumult I could make sure that I was cutting the rope. I redoubled my forces. Ultimately I put half my weight on the knife, then pulled. More noise from below. Then something snapped! That instant I lost my balance. But I had sense enough to throw away the knife as I fell from the tree. In a moment I was sinking in the river—down, down, down. . . .

When I came to the surface of the water again, my face was almost against the thick and double bamboo bars of the cage in which writhed a huge grey-black mass of flesh. I looked more carefully. Yes, he had swallowed those two horns that had stuck out of his mouth when first we located him under the tree. That seemed to satisfy some strange curiosity in me. Another thing I noticed was the size of the brute. He must have been at least a foot in diameter. People around me said that they had never seen a python so large before. However, they were so glad that he was caged and ready to be sold to a museum that, except the priest and Kuri, no one interested himself in me, dripping, choking and bruised.

IV—Initiation Into the Jungle Mystery

AFTER our adventure with the python, Purohit became deeply interested in me. One day he came to our house seeking an interview with my aunt. It was a cold December afternoon so they repaired to the roof of the house. This may seem strange to America but I will explain.

Our house was one of the few situated at the northern end of the village. It was built of stone and mud and its colour through a hundred years of rain and sun had become russet. The beams and rafters were of teak wood. The ceilings were very high. Almost all the houses in India are built to withstand heat; high ceilings and spacious rooms are what is needed to give comfort to a people who have to endure steady tropical heat six months every year, and so winter which lasted about four months was most uncomfortable. We had no fire save outside in the centre of the walled compound, and we had to depend on shawls and woolen wrappers to give us warmth whether in or out of doors. You can judge of our hardships by the fact that every night of the winter the cold was intense enough to freeze water. However, during the day wherever the sun shone it was comfortable, but if you stepped out of the sun into the shade, the cold pierced you like the claw of a panther.

Apparently what the priest had to say to my aunt that December afternoon concerned me, for I was soon invited to join them on the roof. I walked out of my room down the pillared verandah till I reached the stairway at the end, for all staircases in the olden times were placed, not through, but at one of the ends of a house. You had to come out of all the rooms in order to reach them. Next to them came the high outer walls that surrounded the building and the front yard.

When I reached the top, I found the two old people holding a deep conversation. The sky above was blue, the forests not far off were green and russet as usual in the winter, and away in the distant north stood the Himalayas wrapped in winter haze like a tall mirror on which someone had breathed.

The priest looked up and smiled through his white beard. He said: "We are thinking of initiating you." My aunt's face, I noticed as I sat down, looked troubled. Though she was sixty years old, her face had no wrinkles of worry. There were a few lines of age. It seems nowadays that people worry, and their faces are scarred by lines. In India even now the common people don't look hunted and hard, and in the old days they rarely looked excited, so those new lines on Kuri's face filled me with unrest. As if she had divined what was passing in my mind, she remarked, her dark eyes tranquil and steady: "The priest says that you should be initiated by the time you are nine years old."

"You know that you are from the warrior-caste, Kshatryia. The highest caste in India is the Brahmin, that of the priests. The second is yours, that of the soldier. The third is of the tradesmen and farmers who are called Vaisyas. The fourth is the day labourer, the Sudra. This caste system is an accretion of our religion, but it is not coeval with our central belief, and already it is breaking down in the cities. In fifty years it will break up in the country, but in the meantime, as usual, you, a country lad, must undergo the initiation of your caste. Instead of waiting till you are fourteen, you should be initiated before you are ten, for your character is ripe." Then followed a pause when Kuri added further: "You have already served well as a Sudra (day labourer). You have herded the cattle most efficiently. Also you're a gem of a Vaisya. Last spring, you helped in the tillage. You are equipped to be a good farmer. I always dreamt of farming for you. But the priest says that you ought to become a warrior. Why so early, I cannot make out."

Neither could I. So I looked at the priest. He smiled again which disarmed my mind of all questioning. He said: "Come to the temple every morning with the flowers as you have done the past year, but instead of going to the field, spend a couple of hours with me. That is all."

Now the Brahmin rose to take his leave. We saluted him by bowing our heads to the ground. After saying "Swasthu," the usual formula meaning "May your longings be fulfilled," he departed. We sat on the roof and kept silent until the temple bells afar hailed the coming of the night.

Instead of being initiated at nine, I waited until my eleventh year, learning in the meanwhile the craft of a warrior. I spent a great deal of time at the temple, and as month succeeded month my attachment to the priest grew deeper and deeper.

Under his kind guidance I learned that life is one. There is no particular thing that is a favourite of nature and God. Man is not master of all things, but he is one of the servants of Life. This is an example.

One day Purohit and I while walking in the temple gardens encountered a poisonous toad. I raised my stick, in order to destroy it ere it squirted a poisonous liquid from its body which, if allowed to fall on a man's skin, makes it blister with eczema. It was a nasty fellow too, big and strong. No wonder I wanted to despatch him then and there. But Purohit would not let me. He got hold of my stick before I could bring it down on the toad's head. "He may squirt a little poison when you frighten him, but remember, O jewel of wisdom hidden in the ignorance of youth, if thou killest him thou wilt hurt my temple gardens."

"How, my Lord?" I questioned him in wonder.

"Because there are many insects who eat leaves, and worms who eat the blossoms of my growing plants. They are numerous and small. I have no time nor vigilance to track them down, but they must be destroyed if the flowers that we offer for worship are to be perfect, and you know that no one would think of offering worm-eaten blossoms for his adoration of the Divine. Well now, who is it keeps the garden free of insects and worms? It is our friend the toad. And he does not kill them out of malice but devours them to assuage his hunger. He is the best friend that a gardener has and the guardian angel of flowers. Though poets have not yet sung his praise, nor religion built him a shrine, yet the flowers themselves know that he is their friend and saviour. Him unsung, I will not allow you to kill."

Though I was nine years old, these words sank deep into my soul. You cannot destroy one species of animal without upsetting all the balance of life. Life is a whole. There is no escape from this.

Again for instance, if you kill all the snakes, what

would happen? The worms, frogs and creatures they live on would multiply so that they, in order to live, would eat up half the vegetation in the world. Besides, the most important thing in life is its variety. Tigers, elephants, serpents, rhinos, crocodiles, parrots, pigeons, eagles, hawks and peacocks all make for us a splendid spectacle of diversity. If we destroy species after species as we have done in the past, life will be flat, colourless and monotonous, a spectacle of unrelieved dullness. Think of the picturesque vision of a mastodon, a sabre-toothed tiger, or a dinosaurus, stalking through a forest. Does not that quicken the imagination of a boy? Does not that stretch his thinking? Does not that widen the horizon of his mind? So the old proverb is right? "What we can preserve will preserve all."

But the abstract grows from the tree of boredom; monotony hangs like a fruit from its every bough, so I shall eschew it and tell you of the concrete things that Purohit and I did together. Since I came from the warrior caste he taught me the arts of warfare, such as archery, hurling the spear, and wrestling.

Of all these joys, that of archery I will never give up. After I had my first bow made, I went to the blacksmith for my arrows. At last the propitious spring day arrived when I was to be initiated.

My aunt, one of the village elders, Purohit and myself met in the courtyard of the temple where an altar was built and the fire on it was lighted. I had already performed my ablutions and prayers. Kuri took me by the hand and presented me to the priest. She said: "I swear and avow that this my nephew is eager to be initiated into the art of war. He is, I swear, a warrior's son and grandson. In him flows the blood of kings of old who fought for the weak and died to save the helpless. You assembled civilised folk have my word that I wish him to be a Kshatryia, and I permit you to initiate him in the mystery of a warrior's religion."

Then I walked round the sacred fire seven times. That was called Pradakshina. At the end of the Pradakshina I stood facing the priest. He was robed in saffron that flamed in the morning light. Behind him stretched the green lawn and above him hung the sky—a sapphire intangibility. Between us burnt the sandalwood fire. He said: "You come to take initiation of your own accord?" I answered: "Yes, my Lord." That I repeated three times. Next, through his white beard that eagle-eyed Brahmin demanded: "You swear to protect the weak, help the helpless, succour the sufferer and punish the wrong-doer?"

"I swear again and again," I chanted back.

"You will control your passion, you will refrain your senses, you will never hate, nor fear?"

"Yes, my Lord," I agreed.

"He who restrains himself restrains the thunderbolt," went on the priest. "He who draws the blade of insight will not often need the weapon of steel. He who is compassionate shall live without hurting or humiliating others. Will you be humble, my son?"

"Yes, my Lord," I answered.

"Will you be compassionate?"

"Yes, my Lord."

"Will you, instead of controlling others, control yourself first?"

I answered: "I will restrain my senses with all my power."

"Swear again and again," demanded Purohit.

I swore.

Then he lifted from the ground at his feet a bow, a quiver of arrows, and two extra strings. He lifted them above the fire and chanted:

"O fire, purify these weapons,
O sun, sanctify these,
O mother water, wash them clean of all taint of terror and death.
O God within this young man, guide him to use these instruments for the glory of truth, for the safety of the good, and for the reincarnation of your Ancient and Infinite Compassion in the hearts of all men.
Agni Dehi
Agni Dehi
Agni Dehi
Give us the sacrificial fire that purifies
Give us the sacrificial fire that purifies
Give us the sacrificial fire that purifies."

We chanted in unison:

"Swastu Swastu Swastu
So be it so be it so be it."

Purohit chanted his benediction.

Now he handed me the bow and arrows, then led me seven times around the fire. When that last Pradakshina was done, he faced me and said:

"May you live so that all will say about you, he

lived not in vain! May God give me strength to teach you what I know with humility in my heart, purity in my mind, and truthfulness in my soul."

Then I put my hand in Kuri's, and she and I went home together.

When we arrived there a feast had been spread for the whole village to partake of. All castes were present. Even the poor, of whom there were only a few in our village, were at our house in full strength. When we entered, the conch-shells were blown and my head was strewn with flowers by the ladies invited to celebrate the occasion of my initiation.

V—The Art of Hunting

THE ceremony of my initiation had a strange effect upon me. It burnt into my soul that no matter what vocation we choose, it should be considered as a responsibility and not as a holiday. I asked other boys who were initiated into other crafts, and they bore me out in my conclusion. A weaver lad who was initiated a month before me said: " I know now that weaving is not only a vocation but also an adoration of God. I try to make beautiful fabrics to proclaim that I have not scamped my work, nor tried to hoodwink the Invisible."

A carpenter six months after his initiation answered my questions as follows, "I am glad I was put through the ceremony of initiation. I was imposed upon by its solemnity to swear not only to the others present but to myself that I would make beauty and utility for man. I am not afraid to be poor: if my hands are strong and my home free of famine, why should I fret for more riches."

Our Hindu initiation gives courage to the young to live without the fear of poverty. Alas! I had no sister, so I cannot tell you of a young woman's initiation. I witnessed no such event. Now that India is becoming modernised and the time-tested ancient ceremony of initiation is slowly going out of fashion, it would be wise to record all its forms and names for the pleasure of posterity.

Later when I became a hunter by profession, my observation of animal life revealed to me that animals perform their own adoration of the sanctities, and also train and initiate their young.

Adoration of sunset and sunrise among birds and beasts is a common thing. In their eyes the light of the sun is the only God. So when he, the Lord of day arises, eagles wheel at the gates of the east like the ritual dancers in the temple of Nataraja; monkeys sit in silence on tree-tops, even squirrels interrupt their eternal quest for nuts and sit still on their branches till the hour of Light has passed. Sunset too they observe in similar fashion. Religion is necessary both for men and his younger brothers, the dumb souls whose speechlessness is more eloquent than man's speech.

Let me tell you now the tale of an animal's initiation. It was after I was thirty that one day I encountered a family of tigers. The parents were about six years old, and the younglings hardly four months. They were living in the Sunderbans—those beautiful woods of the deltas at the mouth of the Ganges. What a place, the Sunderbans! There the rivers are full of crocodiles and the ground savage with tigers, leopards, panthers and rhinoceros, not to mention wild buffaloes, vipers and tarantulas. The crocodiles were the most dangerous of these, I think, though troubles came from the large cats, and I was appointed by the State to find out why the tigers of the Sunderbans ate man.

I took up my abode in a village of about three score families on the bank of the Ganges. The river was tawny and so broad in those regions that you could hardly see the opposite shore. The village fronted the water as all Hindu settlements do, and behind us, beyond some cultivated land about two miles long and half a mile broad, lay the jungle. The jungle was about ten miles deep, separating us from the village on the other side of the delta. That human habitation was very large and had a weekly boat service to Calcutta about two hundred miles up the sacred river. This village was named Sundari, Beauty.

Our village had the magnificent name of Tajjabpore, Seat of Wonder. It was my duty to accompany the postman of Tajjabpore once a week across the jungle, going on a Tuesday and returning on a Thursday. It was during one of these trips, about the middle of June, that we came across Bagh, his wife Baghini, and their son and daughter. It was a very hot summer and the rain had not yet fallen in large quantities.

During the season of drought, animals, especially deer, elephant and wild buffaloes come near human habitation and assuage their hunger by eating up the growing grain fields. And since every animal follows its food, the big cats followed the vegetarians.

So one Tuesday morning as we crossed the grain fields and entered the woods, we came upon fourfold tiger pugs. Since it was nearly eight in the morning the postman and I concluded that all the tigers were fast asleep by now and it would do us no harm to go on their track. In another twenty minutes we came across a very clear place where the postman said that he saw something moving. We went forward to investigate, and came upon an amazing sight. There lay father and mother tiger on the bank of a small pond not far away. Since the rivers are full of crocodiles, in order to avoid trouble, wild animals generally drink from inland pools that never dry up. The sunlight fell profusely on the waters, and patches of it played on the plants and thorn bushes that framed them.

In order to find out what had happened to the two youngsters we climbed up a tree and looked

That set the monkeys talking
and racing from tree to tree.

down. We distinctly saw the raw skeleton of an animal lying between the parents, and before them about ten feet away, the two cubs were slowly approaching the water's edge to take a drink. It looked as if this was the first time they had gone to the water unaccompanied by Bagh and Baghini for they stepped gingerly: brother, who was the larger of the two, leading sister. They nosed about the shore until they came upon the tracks of the past, and no doubt inferred that since tigers had gone to the drinking place on that path before, the precedent must be adhered to.

First, brother stood over the water, looking about to make sure that no danger presented itself from any direction, then lowering his head—imitating the gestures of an old tiger—he took his drink. Next he turned round, making room for sister. She nosed his ear, as much as to say: "Guard my rear while I drink."

The boy did so with the gallantry of a young gentleman, then they slowly retraced their steps on their previous track to their parents. That display of caution—the sense that one should keep to the old and trusted paths—told me how sagacious young animals generally are.

Now that I had found them, I made up my mind to study as closely as possible the way tigers brought up their young, so I spent the following two months in tracking and watching them. It proved an easy task, for the little ones could not wander very far. The shortness of their legs permitted them no long hunting trips. Even though the monsoon had come and more rain had fallen, yet they stayed between the two villages that lay at either end of the jungle.

The way the parents taught the cubs to hunt was a superb lesson in education. Step by step they were taught. The day they killed their first large calf, I was with them. This was what happened. Towards the end of June it had rained steadily for a whole week. At the end of it when the sun shone again, the cattle of the village went to graze in the forest, for there, like steady green sparks from an anvil, the grass had suddenly shot up. But monsoon weather is freakish. About midday a swift thunderstorm frightened the cows and their herdsmen, and they sped home without waiting to count the heads of the cattle. That is why they did not round up a large calf who was left to find his way home all alone after the storm had passed.

I, who was on a tree during the rain, beheld him straggling along and eating all he could of the tender grass. Suddenly I saw two purple streaks run in the sunlight, and stop facing the poor calf. It was mother tiger and her son. Soon the wind blew the odour of their presence towards the lost creature. He whinneyed almost like a horse as he smelt tiger, and turning round dashed for the jungle. There in the shadows he saw father tiger and daughter. I shouted from the tree top—but too late. A flash of purple, yellow and black—the calf's tail raised stiff in the air—then. . . .

That evening when I returned to Tajjabpore and told the villagers what had happened they scolded me for not saving that poor calf. It never entered their heads that had I come between their food and the four cats, I would not be there to tell the tale! I never shoot an animal, as a rule, except from great necessity, and on this particular afternoon, I had not taken my rifle with me, though as a forest warden of the State I was allowed a gun. I explained to the villagers that tigers, even the born man-eaters, do not kill their first human victim until he comes between them and their prey at a critical moment. But once the tiger has tasted human blood, and learns the helplessness of his prey, he does not hesitate to kill whenever he corners man. Moreover man is a biped: he cannot run away as fast as a deer or any other quadruped, and that makes any human being, without a rifle, helpless before the striped and spotted enemy.

After the killing of that large calf, the village was nervous, and set up special watches for its cattle. As for human beings, none ventured abroad after nightfall. I said, "If a man carries a burning torch or a well-lit hurricane lantern, no beast of prey will go out of its way to meet him. The more you are seen at night, the wider berth they will give our village, but if you do not take the offensive, the animals will become aggressive. They smell fear more quickly than you know, and your fear will frighten them to attack you." But only the postman agreed with me. It was the two of us out of that entire village who ever went abroad at any hour, day or night. Though I always carried a torch, I rarely lighted it. My eyes were extremely keen: in fact the keenest of all the hunters of my time. I could see in the dark better than antelopes. Sometimes I was credited with the eye power of the tiger, so at night, unless I wanted to keep the animals far away, I never carried a flaming torch. So now my eyes had to serve me to the utmost, for I was studying the two cubs and their education at all hours, and they led me into all kinds of places. At first, the parents, I noticed, did all the hunting, though the children stalked the prey and frightened them yet the cubs were not pushed to leap and kill. That final deed the parents shared between them. Watching the parents educated the children considerably, yet in spite of this, the parents took the children to places where it would be possible for them to leap and kill if they wished. One day I saw them do an interesting thing. It was around midday, near the drinking place. The parents and the children were lying wide awake near the pond. The wind was blowing from the opposite direction. Soon at the other end of the pond came a wild buffalo family. Father and mother stood on either side while the young steer, about two months old, drank his fill. Then the father took his drink while the other two watched. Last drank the cow, whose rear the bull and the calf protected. Then the parents lay down, their backs to the water, and before them in the jungle their child grazed and frisked about. From my tree-top I could see mother tiger pushing away her babies from her as if they were too big to be cuddled. So they trotted out, and soon caught the scent of the buffaloes. For awhile I lost sight of them, and then I saw them coming towards the guileless bull calf playing in the grass. Now quickly the cubs crouched and vanished again from sight, but they crawled nearer and nearer, as I could tell from the protruding of their snouts every few seconds from under leaves or saplings here and there. At last they attacked the young steer who mooed for help. Moo! . . . Instantly like two black rocks the cow and the bull charged. Their bellowing filled the jungle with terror. The tiger cubs fled helter-skelter. Why the buffaloes waited so long ere they ran to the protection of their calf I could not make out, but probably they too were educating him as the tigers were educating their young. When the cubs reached home, they looked crestfallen. The daughter went to her father and the boy put his head under his mother's chin.

Another time the young male cub attacked a baby monkey. No sooner had he done so than the father and mother monkeys fell on him like two fiends. They slapped his face so hard that he let go of the baby monkey whose tail his paws had held like a vise. No sooner had he released it than all three of them scurried up a tree and jabbered in terror. That set flocks and flocks of monkeys talking and racing from tree to tree, frightening in their turn birds who were taking their afternoon rest. What a din of screeching birds and howling monkeys!

In the meantime the defeated cub came home to his mother, for that day father and sister had gone off by themselves, and there they lay together near the drinking pond, mother licking and patting him. But on these and several other occasions that followed the parents never interfered nor helped the children. It is the first requisite of a tiger's life that he should tackle his job, whether hunting or wandering, singly. At a certain time, in order to train them in self reliance, the parents put their cubs in the way of work, but nothing more.

At last it rained so hard that I lost sight of them for more than a fortnight. It was about the beginning of August while the postman and I had gone across to the village of Sundari for the mail, that we heard of four tigers there who had killed three head of cattle in a week. This whetted my curiosity, and as soon as the mail was received the postman and I set out for the jungle. It did not take us long to find and recognise the family. The cubs had grown by now, the boy was almost as high as the mother, though not as long, his footprints resembled hers so closely that you could not distinguish them. Only one thing betrayed the cub, his step was not so long as the mother's. She took much wider strides. So when we saw two sets of identical pugs, with four in each of greater compass, we concluded that mother and son walked beside each other, while the daughter invariably kept the company of her father.

Having sighted their lairs, I went back to Tajjabpore with the postman. Then I hastened back to my four striped beasts. They moved ever closer to our village. In a couple of days they had come perilously close to it. As they emerged from the thick jungle I perceived that all was not going well with the family. The father was becoming increasingly jealous of the son. Every time the mother's back was turned, the old fellow attacked the boy with the intent to kill. At one time he came so close to slashing the boy's throat with his paw that the latter yelled for help. Then from nowhere leaped mother between them, and attacked her husband. They fought and fought, but at last she won. After that severe tussle he ran away—never to be seen again.

Her job was now doubly difficult; she had to kill both for her two children and herself. But you know a tigress! She took no half measures; she forced the boy to fill his father's place, and he had to go and stalk the prey while mother waited at a given point to leap and kill.

One afternoon close to nightfall they changed plan. She and daughter did the stalking. They brought a big buffalo up to him and lo, he leaped! But instead of falling on its neck, he fell on its rear, and with a terrific kick of his legs the black bull cleared himself and ran. Not one of the three could catch him, so that night they went without food. Next evening the same thing happened, but when on the fourth occasion the mother and daughter drove up to him half a dozen big buffaloes whom he could not attack, the mystery of the situation cleared. She was giving him his last lesson. After this the family would break up, so he must learn to stalk and kill all by himself. What was most surprising, she was giving him the hardest thing to do first, but by failure at the great one he was learning the easier tasks with infallible power and skill. How different that is from our human way of training people, with the easiest always first. In nature animals cannot afford such long drawn-out step-by-step training. Animal children cannot be segregated in the schoolroom from the sharp experiences of life. They have to be educated in the heart of life itself. The easy and the difficult befall them without any sequence. It is a pity that in civilisation man has made the business of education so sequestered and slow.

However, to return to our tiger reaching his final initiation. I have already intimated that all three of them had gone without food for four days. Hunger was tearing their vitals. They were so famished that they curtailed their daylight sleep. Sister and brother, the fifth day, killed a baby monkey at the water hole. But it could not assuage their hunger. Late that afternoon when the sun was setting, they came out towards our village on the river bank and sat there looking at the bars of light vibrate and die on the high waters of the night of the full moon. In the village men and women sang as they finished their day's work, and Papias (Indian thrushes) sang in the sky—pa . . . . p . . i . . a . . ! The green jungle throbbed like an emerald cast in a garnet crucible.

How swiftly the tropical twilight passes! In a half hour the moon had risen, sending currents of cold white fire through the waters and every bough of the trees. The three beasts of prey prowled around the village. But no cattle had gone astray, and men carrying torches were the only living creatures who passed and repassed on the roads. One of these men was myself. Seeing us, the tigers retreated from the village into the woods. I too went thither after putting out my torch, but circuitously. Hardly had I reached the edge of the jungle than I heard something start. With the celerity of an ape I went up a tree, and looking down I saw a milk-white buck going to graze on the ripe crop of the fields. Save his horns, the most of him was lost in the tall rice plants whose tops shivered in silver dance rhythms as he pushed through them. The moonlight was so bright that most animals could not sleep. Talk, talk, talk of birds and beasts rang like an insistent hammering on every nerve centre of one's body.

Slowly appeared against the wind a pair of emeralds. It was a tiger's eyes. He came up rapidly towards the rice crop in which the buck had buried himself. But all the time he kept closely under the shadow of the jungle. His purpose was to approach gradually until he reached the spot exactly behind the stag which would cut off the latter's retreat. Those green eyes grew larger, then vanished. In a short time an odour of tiger, carried up by the slow breeze, told me that he was crouching under my tree. I knew because of the jungle noises that the greedy buck, lost in rice-eating, had not heard his approach. Afar off on the other side were coming down wind four green eyes. In a short time the stag sensed the odour of tiger. He turned round and dashed for the jungle. Alas, poor brother—that moment from almost six feet away leaped a silvery flash which coiled itself around and hung from his neck. In two more minutes his throat was torn, and life had oozed out of him. Just then mother and sister leaped forward and claimed their share of the booty. But they were greeted with a sky-rending roar from the boy, that said: "It is my kill. I did it all alone. I am the Master! I am the King!" Mother had apparently had previous experience in initiating children. She thrust a paw at sister who still insisted on claiming her share, and stilled her whining; then the two of them slunk away out of sight.

After he had eaten his fill, the cub roared and yelled as he went in the direction of the water hole. His cry of triumph told all the world that he had graduated from school. The far off panic-stricken echoes shouted, "Here comes the King of the beasts."

Now mother and daughter emerged from the shadows and fell upon the remains of the dead buck. They ate long and well. After all, they had to feed the hunger of nearly a week.

From that night on, we saw no more triple pug marks. For several days we noticed a solitary tiger's track in the deep jungles, and the other two, the mother and daughter, went in the opposite direction, no doubt looking for father near some village up the river. Thus ends the story of a tiger's initiation. Not only they, but all other animals perform a series of rites which teaches them self-control and self-reliance with which they may be trusted to live their life.

VI—Life of a Hindu Village

THE priest, after my initiation, began to explain to me the symbols of our religion and the truths that lie hidden under the rituals of our daily observances. He told me that each man should prepare for his day's work in his sleep of the preceding night.

Does this seem strange? Let me explain. Early one morning he and I went hunting. I carried a javelin, and he a cudgel. Our objective was to find a fish-eating eagle's nest where the eggs must have been laid now that it was the beginning of April. It took six hours steady climbing toward Ladak before we reached a blue lake on whose shore rose titanic cliffs, white as chalk. There we decided to eat luncheon. So Purohit took out of his wallet fried corn (pop-corn) saturated with butter and salt.

Then we went to the lake to drink. I stood on a ledge, then bending down drank of the blue water. On my retreating back to where we stood, the priest went forward to take his drink. While he was bending over monkey-fashion, I looked up at the sky. A black point plunged down from it, getting bigger and bigger every second. It was like the falling of a black rock. Behind it followed another exactly like it. There was no more doubt in my mind that those two eagles had seen Purohit and were pouncing to kill him by burying their talons in his neck. That instant I rose to my feet and balanced my javelin. I was acting as I was expected to act in stories that depict fights between men and eagles.

One of the eagles fell, making the air shriek and whistle over the entire lake. He fell about twenty feet away from Purohit. But the one that followed seemed to aim at his head. Its winging the air was more fierce sounding: the chalky cliffs resounded with the echoes of it. Down, down, down it fell. Fearing that in an instant it would fall on the priest's neck, I hurled my javelin. Lo! It made a thud-like noise. Then the eagle opened one wing and shrieked. . . . I shall never forget that fatal sound. It was the very voice of Death. He made a weary semi-circle in the air, then sank into the lake. In the meantime the first eagle rose in the air with a large fish held in its talons. But that it let fall as soon as it saw its mate drowning below.

The priest came running at me, shouting with indignation, his hair and beard wet and dripping: "Why did you kill the poor eagle?"

"My Lord, that bird was going to fall on you," I answered.

"How outrageous! They have known me for years. They came down to catch fish, not to kill me."

Just then the mate of the dying eagle shrilly cried and circled the air, almost touching the water where the other's wing still rose and fell like the fan of a weary windmill. Ah, God! what had I done! The cliffs and their echoes clanged with the wail of the husband who beat the lake surface with his wings—alas, in vain. At last the wounded bird ceased lifting its wing, and the water dragged it down into its depth. Now her maddened mate shrieked like a lunatic and flew all over the place looking for us. But the priest had already drawn me with himself under a tree. Thence we could still see the male eagle searching for his enemy.

About half an hour later, seeing her dead body float on the water, he gave up all hope and flew up to his eyrie over the cliffs clear out of sight. Purohit rebuked me: "Those are fish-eating eagles. They have never hurt any other animals. I have known them since they were mere babies. This is the fifth year that I have made my pilgrimage to their nest. Alas! they, that is he, will never return hither. They never revisit the scenes of death once they go away. Next year there will be no eagles in that eyrie."

I was so heartsick at my murderous blunder that I could hardly speak. The priest sensed my feelings and he spoke no more. He went back to the ledge, took off his tunic, and with his dhobi, loin-cloth, tightly tied on himself, plunged into the water.

In the inland lakes or the rivers of the interior there are no crocodiles or other killers. He swam safely to the heart of the lake, caught the dead bird's wing between his teeth, and swam back to the shore.

It was too heavy for him to carry. So while I dragged it away from the end of the ledge, Purohit climbed up and came to my assistance. We deposited the bird on a large rock. Then, after he had put on his tunic, the two of us gathered a lot of dry twigs and leaves in order to cremate it properly. Now began the funeral rites. I walked around the pyre singing:

"Akasastu riralamba bayu bhuta rirashraya"

"Now thou art homeless on the earth, houseless on the water, no abode for thee in the air, so liberated go forth, O soul, O immortal reality, to the House of Song and join the company of the light-vestured gods."

We lighted the fire by striking stone upon stone. Soon the dry leaves crackled and smoked. In two hours time the bird was cremated. Now we chanted the last words:

"Seek not thy vesture of flesh—go thither where the sons of immortality await thee."

That was as good as a human funeral. But you must bear in mind that we Hindus believe that not only man but animals too have souls. If at death men's souls have to be prayed and chanted into immortality, why not those of the beasts? It is inconvenient to observe the funeral rites of all dying animals. But we can observe some in order to remind ourselves that the soul is immortal and cannot die with the body. In a few minutes the widowed eagle returned. He flew over the water. As soon as the wind was heard singing through his wings like the storm in the reeds, the fish that had been jumping on the water became still and sank way down to the water's depths. But he, the hunter of heights, had no thought of killing. He was scanning and hovering over the water for one more glimpse of his beloved. At that sight a keen pain slashed my feelings. Unable to bear it, I burst into tears. On our return home the priest said: "I will leave you with your aunt. After I finish my evening work at the temple I shall come back to see you. Do not go to sleep until I come back!"

About half past nine he came to the roof where I lay on a mat, for the night was hot, and sat near my head and spoke thus: "Let no pain-memory go with you into the house of sleep. No unhappy thoughts should ride on the back of your mind while you journey into the mansion of sleep. You have done neither right nor wrong, you are God's child. May He usher you into the grotto of unconsciousness. No fear, no sorrow, no remorse. You are perfect, you are the chalice of serenity and Ananda, Bliss." Thus he talked. Each sentence erased from my heart the scar after scar of gloomy thinking and self-reproach. At last, listening to his humming speech I felt drowsy. All that I remember now is the eyes of the listening stars, that slowly pushed me off the ledge of consciousness into a fathomless expanse of sweet murmuring.

A week later when he was teaching me the Mahabharata he said: "Never go to sleep with bad thoughts and torturing memories. They will not help you to wake up whole and fully serene—the two states of mind and body without which no man can acquit himself well at his day's task. A child should be ushered into the chamber of sleep with serene joy."

VII—Drought

THE first person in the village of Mayavati to rouse herself from sleep was always my aunt. Day after day, month on month, year after year, the thud of her bare feet on the village road marked the beginning of morn for every villager. They knew by the sound of her slow walk that it was she who was going to bathe in the river. She returned home exactly when the sun was leaping off a peak of the

Himalayas. Even when the sky was veiled with clouds our village surmised that the sun had risen because Kuri had returned from her ablutions of the morning. In India all the hours of the day have their rituals, the day-break first of all. In Mayavati the summer days are not as long as in the valley, owing to the high Himalayan peaks that cast their shadows on us from the northeast and west. In the winter on the contrary when the sun goes south, the days are longer.

Winter or summer the day's ritual rarely varied. Most of the villagers awoke during the last hour of the night, performed their ablutions, and then, before the sun swung over the diamond peaks of the Himalayas, prayed and meditated at least half an hour. The prayers they said were numerous, but under all of them ran the perpetual rhythm of the same thought,

"O energy of repose in my heart,
O compassionate Silence
Lead me from the unreal to the real,
From darkness into Light,
From death into Immortality!
Make me so serene that I may be stiller than the hills
And also swifter than the swiftest flight of man's mind
Anejadeko manasajabiya!
Kamasya yatrapta Kamastatra
mam amritam Krisi
Where longings have been quieted, there make me live."

After meditation was over, boys of my age went to the house of the Pulwan Lathiwal, our teacher of wrestling and fencing. (Pulwan means wrestler, and

Lathiwal, fencer.) He was a clean shaven athlete of about thirty whose duty it was to teach wrestling and fencing to the youngsters of the village. He taught all castes, at all times and in any kind of group. Under the thatched roof of his open pavilion lay the silt from the bed of the river Avati, which had been dried and pounded till it had become soft as cotton. On that soil-mattress, dressed in Jangiyo or tight shorts, we wrestled with one another and with Pulwan Lathiwal. Lads have wrestled thus from time immemorial in India, and it is generally called Kusthi.

As we came out from the Kusthi exercises and went to the river to wash off the dust and grime therein, the day had generally begun in earnest. The herdsmen drove their cattle to the field; the tiller clicked his tongue and urged his bullocks to pull the plough: crows, kites and hawks flew far away in the heavens, while men set to work at their separate tasks. The weaver fretted at the tearings of the thread that he wove, the potter grumbled at the dry clay under his hand, and the smith wondered why it was so hard to work at his forge. In the meantime the cows lowed a distinct foreboding, and the horses neighed their distaste for toil. Purohit, who had felt a premonition of what was coming, said as he gave me my lessons: "The dry season has begun, maybe we shall have a terrible drought this year. Let God avert the bolt of calamity from this land!" But without doubt misfortune was upon us. Each day the heat grew more and more unbearable as the sun rose higher in the sky. Yet work went on. The cowherds blew their flutes as if they were gods playing in a grove. The ploughmen sang thus:

> "How shall I stay at home and mind the fire
> When I hear the flutings of my love?"

The weaver who was working at a saffron bridal veil softened his threads with this chanting:

> "O my friend, I could not see him well! Through my veil I looked at my beloved, I could not see him well. In the breast of the cloud the lightning scorches and escapes. How can I tell you of him, for I am blinded by seeing his face."

As for the blacksmith in spite of the din and clamour of steel on steel, he too sang as he wrought hard iron into the flowing designs of beauty:

> "Hammer and anvil
> Sing, brothers, sing!
> Tame the tongue of iron red,
> Its eyes of scarlet,
> Its body—a flint.
> Tame, tame, tame,
> Sing, and shape,
> Hammer and anvil
> This iron red."

The potter is bending over a large wheel at least two feet in diameter, resting at its centre on a spoke about three inches high. We see only his turban of ochre, his brown body wrapped in a white coat, and his limbs covered with white payjama—a Hindu word meaning "paya" or legs, "jama" covering, in short trousers. His long sensitive fingers are on the clay dug from the bottom of the river when the water is very low. He is piling the clay about a foot high on the wheel at its centre. Now that is done, he twirls the wheel. It turns slowly at first, then with gathering momentum it spins faster and faster. Now he presses it with slight touches here and there till the whole thing spins on an even keel. Feeling sure that all is ready he puts his two thumbs on the clay at the centre and presses on it. Like magic the clay blossoms into a cup. Quickly he takes a wet thread lying in a cup of water on the ground, and applies it under the new-born cup. It goes on spinning as if it had not been separated at all from the rest of the clay. The potter with his two fore-fingers touches and slows down his wheel a little, then deftly lifts up the full-fledged cup with his hand as a fancier lifts a tame dove from its nest. He puts it down in the sun, and then twirls his wheel again, but instead of making his second cup blossom quietly under his thumbs, he sings to its clay matrix:

"Lilies on water,
Stars in the sky,
The curve of a bird-wing,
The grace of a bride,
Come all, come—
And abide in the cups
that I build!"

In the temple the priest went on explaining to me addition, subtraction and all the other mysteries of numbers. What he told me about them you know. For instance, he said that all the so-called Arabic numerals that the whole world uses are not Arabic at all, they were invented by the ancient Hindus. In the seventh century A.D., the Arabs, when they came to India, learnt them from the Hindus and took along with them the decimal system of notation to Europe and gave them to the Christian nations. Without that two-fold product of Hindu genius, mathematical science would not have progressed so rapidly.

But I was most interested in the priest's story of the origin of the decimal system. Purohit said: "You notice how natural it is to count up to ten, and then stop? That system of ten man did not get from looking at the sky. He got it by looking at himself."

"What do you mean, my Lord?" I question in bewilderment.

Purohit answered: "Count your fingers. How many are there?"

"Ten, my Lord."

"How many toes have you?" he asked again.

I answered, "Ten, my Lord."

"Well," continued the priest, "it is the recurrence of ten that amazed the ancient Hindus. You know, my son, men counted on their fingers then as they do now, and every time they did so they either counted up to ten or to a fraction thereof. In the dim past, there was a clever man who noted down what he counted. He made marks on the ground with a stick and any counting that did not come up to ten he put down as a fraction, or part of ten: a mark—decimal before it. That is how the decimal system originated along with the numerals in ancient India. The only thing we should thank the old Hindus for is that they knew how to use their fingers."

The story of my education under Purohit would fill a volume. But the instance of the numerals shows how he presented science, whether the science of mathematics, or any other branch of study. My training was a mixture of meditation, science, scriptures, and literature.

At about eleven the artisans and the workers stopped their work. The increasing heat of the April day drove schoolboy and labourer to bathe in the river. But no Hindu walks directly into the water, for that would be sacrilege. We would sit down on the water's edge, scoop up some of it and pray thus:

> "No matter what your colour or quality, I pray that you be as sacred and blessing-laden as the seven sacred rivers. O Mother, permit me to bathe in you."

After that prayer, I plunged into the water. O, it felt so refreshingly cool! The river was very shallow and its current not swift, so I went across, just for fun. But on the other side I saw something that made me pause and think. Along the river lay pugs of tigers, not one but many, before them the spoor of elephant had marked the ground, and there were footprints of other beasts too. At the sight of them I felt as thrilled as a doctor who finds out a cure for new sickness. Instead of telling anybody anything, I recrossed the river, performed my ablution and went home. I meant to keep my discovery to myself until meeting Purohit the following afternoon.

When I reached home I changed my clothes, then went into our family chapel and meditated for a quarter of an hour, listening to the noonday silence. Is there anything more awe-inspiring than the heat of a tropical noon vibrating like a stinging harp string?

Our dinner began with lentil soup. After that Kuri and I had rice cooked in water and seasoned with butter, and curried potatoes and egg plants fried in ghee (clarified butter). For dessert we had curd and sugar. To the Hindu eating is something in the nature of a sacrament. In hotels we eat alone in our rooms; at home we eat one or two at a time, and talk very little.

Today, however, I had to speak; I had to tell my aunt all that I had seen. She listened in silence through the meal to my sentences between the courses. After dinner was over, as I lay down in my room for the siesta she came over to speak her mind, saying:

"I saw the animals pass the river bank very early this morning when I went to bathe."

"No!" I exclaimed in amazement.

"Yes. Now that you have seen their foot-prints let us watch them pass tonight."

"Are you serious, Kuri?"

"Yes, my child," she reassured me. "I promise to take you with me."

"But how do you know they will come back?" I asked, fearing that the animals would not return, the very thought filling me with disappointment.

"There will be others. The numerous foot-prints that you saw indicate that the animals are going down stream because the drought has dried up the springs of the hills. Last night only the vanguard passed by our village. Many more herds will follow. No fear, we shall see them all tonight. Now rest, O beloved of blessedness!"

But I could not rest. Those animals going by our village proved too much for my imagination, their long procession was marching across my brain and yet I had to wait till nightfall to witness their exodus seawards.

The life of our village went on that afternoon as if nothing uncanny was in the air, and I, who knew what was in store for us, went about my business as if nothing had happened or was going to happen. About three in the afternoon, the heat relented, and I went to play with the boys of our village. Though I was a friend of all of them, yet I kept aloof from them, and very rarely told them of my adventures. Even to this day though many people like me, and I love most of them, yet I cannot unburden my soul and mind into their hearing. There is always something that I keep entirely to myself, and that is why from time to time human beings misunderstand me.

On that particular afternoon we played Keet Keet, Danda Gooli, and Lathi. Keet Keet is a simple game, in its essence it is a primitive form of American football without a ball. It is played on an open field of the size and nature of a tennis court, where the place of the net is taken by a white line drawn on the turf. After the marking of the field into two sections the next thing we did was to divide ourselves into two teams, the Reds and the Blues. Now the rule of the game is that if a Red crosses the line to the other side and is made captive by the Blues he is counted out as dead. Imagine the amount of wrestling a single individual has to do with a whole flock of boys in order to free himself and get home to his own team alive!

Now after we had divided ourselves into Reds and Blues and occupied our respective courts as the toss up indicated, one of ours, myself a Red, had to cross over shouting Keet Keet, meaning catch me if you can and hold me until I admit defeat. I must say my shouting and bragging could not be backed up very long by wrestling. The nine Blues fell upon me like an avalanche of humanity and sat on head, neck, and trunk, till I admitted defeat. Now that I was counted dead I sat on the edge of the court and rooted for our team. A Blue came over to our side of the court shouting, Keet Keet. Our men did their best to grapple with him. Alas, he dragged himself away from them and returned a victor to his team. For that achievement of this Blue another Red was counted out as dead. No doubt the loss of two of its members at the outset told upon the resistance of our team. In fifteen more minutes all the Reds were dead and the Blues triumphant and cheering.

After that game we began Gooli Danda. This consisted of hitting a piece of wood about three inches long with a stick about a foot long. Keet Keet is a form of Rugby, and Gooli Danda a primitive kind of baseball or cricket. The gooli, or little piece of wood, is thick in the middle, and has two fine tapering ends. It is laid on the ground at a given wicket, and then one boy takes the danda (bat, as it were), the foot long stick, in his hand and aims at the gooli. Our batsman struck one end of it, and ball-like it rose in the air flying and twirling like a top. If anyone missed hitting it while it lay on the ground, he lost his chance and became a dunce, but if nobody missed, the one whose hit sent it the shortest distance from the wicket became the dunce.

I happened to be the dunce on this particular afternoon. Each one of the nineteen boys stood at the wicket and hit the gooli in the air, and I had to catch it before it reached the ground. Such is the punishment for a dunce. If I failed my next chance of winning out would be to throw back the gooli from where it fell at the wicket and hit the danda that lay on the ground. If I failed again, then the same boy who had hit the gooli last would pick it up and send it flying through the air again with a stroke of the danda. Well, half an hour before sundown I caught the gooli coming down through the air the nineteenth time. I was nearly exhausted!

From the fields we hastened to the house of Palwan Lathiwal. There twenty boys divided into ten pairs and fenced first with Chota Lathi, small staves, about two feet and a half long, for twenty minutes. Before the British became rulers of India, the Chota Lathi was practised by masked men with swords, but since then the country has been disarmed and now we fence with sticks. In the art of stroke and parry I was quite an adept. Our teacher Palwan Lathiwal watched each pair carefully, and if anyone made a mistake he corrected him at once. After the Chota Lathi was over, we took up the real Lathi, which were brass-shod rods about six feet long. The chota could be wielded with one hand, but the bara, or big lathi, could be lifted only with two. Now began the battle royal. Ten boys, brandishing the big sticks attacked ten more similarly armed. It reminded me of a riot, but with a few bruises on our bodies and several bumps on our hands, we finished lathi altogether for the day.*

Now came the hour of prayer. We went to the temple nearby, washing hands, faces and feet, and thence to the outer chapel to meditate on infinite tranquillity. This is something that all boys and girls must do in India.

Purohit, our priest, sat facing us all and chanted in Sanskrit to Silence:

> "Yasyantam navidu sura suragana
> Devaya tasmai namo
>
> O, thou fathomless Light whom not even
> the gods can describe, we salute Thee!"

Each one of us tried to conceive of Life in this wise. I said to myself: "All is tranquil. Animals, men, birds—all are tranquil. I too am tranquil. May my tranquillity become so great that whatever I touch will become serene. What I feel is calmly felt. What I think is calmly thought. What I do shall be charged with calm.

> Calm Calm Calm
> Peace Peace Peace
> Peace be unto all!"

* The rules of this game are too elaborate to give them all here in detail.

Then I began to listen to Silence. Though that is difficult, one must try. Let me illustrate the art of hearing silence. Suppose you are in the country listening to all the sounds. If you are attentive you will hear every sound in various tones. The wind, for instance, does not make the same noise when it shakes a pine tree as when it trembles through the leaves of a poplar and when it sighs among the reeds it strikes our ears differently from when it breathes upon the water. But if you think you have heard the farthest reach of the wind stilling itself in the distance you are mistaken. It may be almost inaudible when it shivers on the calm surface of the lake, but yet it can be heard. You must go deeper till you can hear it hover like a dragon-fly in its even flight. Sometimes I have heard the wind far off like the tremble of a piece of gauze; then as I meditated deeper, that stopped suddenly and silence rose like a fountain from the void.

Have you ever heard silence? It is not stillness which is the absence of sound. Silence is not empty, it is full of content. It is like the sky—intangible yet containing the stars, the sun, the moon, and all existence. That is Silence and it is full of tongues.

When our meditation was over, the priest blessed us, and we went to our respective homes. After supper consisting of chapati (very much like tortilla, Mexican bread) soaked in butter, eaten with beans, seasoned with curry powder and with mangoes for dessert, Kuri and I went to the temple to hear the epic Mahabharata read and explained by Purohit. Men and gods war with each other in that epic. It was the story of the battle of Titans and the gods this evening with the special episode known as Garuda,* the Thunder-bird, stealing the secret of Immortality from Heaven. It was a most thrilling story. I did not know how time passed.

The majority of the Hindus still go to the temples in the evening to hear the epics, in much the same fashion as the Americans go to the movies. Though my mind was full of the animals passing by our village, yet the story from the epic was rendered with such art by the priest that it held my attention completely and I forgot all about everything else for the time being. The tale of stealing the secret of Immortality from the gods is not only dramatic but universal, and appears, I am told, in the epics of other nations as well as ours.

At last the reading was over and after the priest had blessed the congregation, Kuri and I slipped out into the dry windy night. In India from the end of February the wind blows from the south, and very rarely from any other direction until after August. That particular night was not exceptional, which was very fortunate for us, for since Kuri had planned to stay on the northern shore of the river the animals who were likely to pass would get no wind of us. If anyone were to receive the scent it would be ourselves. After searching about the all too familiar hither shore, we at last found a screen of trees, and below them larches that made a perfect screen for us. There we sat down comfortably and listened for sounds from the opposite

* Garuda is the Hindu equivalent of Prometheus.

bank whose vague outline we perceived before us.

Suddenly we heard something growl behind us. I almost jumped forward into the river, but Kuri, who had great presence of mind, grabbed my hand and restrained me. She said: "That is a man coughing—maybe it is the priest, bent on the same errand as ourselves."

"Yes," a voice said near us: "I too wish to see the animals." There was no mistaking the priest's voice now.

"Come and sit near us," said my aunt. "But don't go coughing about this place and startling men and beasts."

"I saw them pass last night, so I thought—" began Purohit, sitting down beside me. You know animals in nature are not stupid enough to perform as punctually as do their tamed brothers in a circus. The priest, next to him myself, and then my old aunt, sat in a row waiting for the show to begin. Nothing happened. Even the wind grew tired of waiting and almost fell asleep, and I, unable to ward off slumber any longer, put my head on Kuri's lap and sank into sleep. I know not how long I had slept when I was gently shaken. It did not have to be repeated; in a trice my whole being was all attention. I sat up while I was opening my eyes, but what they saw was disappointing, only a stretch of empty field surrounded by trees that stood out like a wall of stiff paper in the light of the risen half moon. Apart from its light, nothing new had come on the stage before us. I made a gesture of disgust and prepared to lie down again.

But the priest whispered, "Listen, something is stirring in the stillness far off."

I listened carefully, but received no impression whatsoever.

My aunt remarked very softly, "Elephants—they walk so quietly!"

I, who had stretched my hearing to the finest point, heard nothing but the shiver of the dying wind on the water and the tiniest throb of the tassels on the larch. Nothing, nothing more.

But that something was happening in the dark forest to the west there was no doubt. There was a tension in the air, which moved eastward. Like curtains parting imperceptibly the darkness parted to our right, and then like a scene in a theatre stood before us a mammoth tusker. How still he stood—as if he were carved out of black marble. The moonlight on his trunk flashed like a column of white water, and his tusks, which must have been very long, looked white as the moon itself. That stone-still figure slowly took on motion. Have you ever seen a vast Banyan tree slowly assume colour at dawn? Then you can imagine how motion touched and quickened that colossal immobility. He raised his trunk to the moon whose light ran like roots of a tree gripping a granite rock. Streaks of moonlight slid down his front legs. The entire mass before us now became charged with energy. He flung his trunk far forward to sniff the air, then to right and left. "No," he seemed to say to himself, "no odour of danger in any direction,—better move on!"

Swiftly the creature, as massive as a temple,

moved and vanished. And just where it had emerged into sight a few moments before stood a big female elephant. She walked on followed by a young tusker. Thus they passed, one after the other—an entire herd. Hardly had they gone when a very large male elephant emerged, of exceptional height. Though he appeared a straggler, there was no doubt that he was the second chief of the herd, and the first one's business was to lead, the last tusker's duty lay in protecting the rear of the flock from any attack. One could tell this by his peculiar gesture of flinging his trunk backward on the right and on the left which meant that he was inhaling the air behind him to make sure that no danger was dogging the footsteps of the herd. Like a dream dreamt, he too was gone.

But their passage had transfigured the river bank, as if the holy of holies had traversed the space before us and left it charged with majesty and wonder. There was a feeling of tension in the air. Hours seemed to have passed when an enormous sambur (a deer as big as a bull) stalked out of the west and stood before us. As if they were treading a line made straight under their feet deer after deer followed him eastward, quiet and calm without any fear in them at all. The only thing that made their march memorable was the flash of moonlight that fell on their muzzles as each one stepped out of the forest shadows at the west.

An utterly eventless half hour passed and then came a quick snap, snap, snap from the west and lo, a tiger and tigress were drawing their sinuous path on the shore! A shiver of terror and pleasure seized us. I put one hand in Kuri's and the other in Purohit's, and squeezed them hard. In spite of the reassuring pressure from both of them, I was unable to control my fear and enjoyment, for it was my first vision of wild tigers. Like a hypnotised creature my eyes were riveted on the other bank of the river long after they had gone. It seemed to me that no time had elapsed before another pair of felines had come and with lightning like speed disappeared from west to east. Whether they were leopards or tigers was hard to tell.

Now took place the most poignant scene of the night. The moon had already risen towards its meridian when half a dozen boars and then buffaloes passed. Following them came a small herd of elephants. But they were very noisy. The snapping of twigs, and crackling of dry leaves rent the air with explosive sounds as they descended from the river bank to the slender rill at its centre to take a drink. They grunted and complained at the mud in which their feet sank. After they had drunk their fill, they quieted down, and slowly one by one they climbed back on to the bank. The way they put up their forefeet, and dragged up their heavy hind feet was a study in leverage, as faultlessly functioning as perfectly built smooth machinery.

But the noises that they had hitherto made they ceased to repeat, as if some majestic presence had awed and silenced their animal senses. We too felt an awe-compelling reverence for something approaching. A palpitating stillness possessed animals, trees, and human beings. Slowly and inevitably some intangible yet adamantine weight descended down the air.

Two stars set, one after the other like candles snuffed out.

The elephants lifted their trunks as if in salutation. Just then a Doel (Indian nightingale) gave out a piercing cry of joy, that ran zig-zagging like chain lightning through a granite stillness. As implements of magic are gathered up in the wizard's wallet, the elephant herd slipped out of sight into the copse to the left.

And the day broke a fountain of gold in the east.

VIII—Human Beings and the Drought

THE heat went on increasing from day to day. Our river, Avati, dried up rapidly and became so slender that she was not broad enough for "the leap of a boy." Animals of the jungle went by our village in the early mornings and late afternoons utterly unmindful of the presence of man as well as oblivious of hurt and harm from one another. Leopards could be seen preceding a herd of antelopes by a few hundred yards. Boars and wolves led one another on their eastward journey as if they were members of the same family. Now and then bisons took their siesta on the village threshing floor under the cooling canopy of the banyan tree. It is well known that different species of animals act as if they were members of the same family in the face of a common danger. Whether it be forest fire, flood or drought, they face it not singly but as a group. Not only do elephants co-operate with the fleeing weasels, but panthers aid the wild buffaloes and herons show the way to sparrows on whom they prey in normal times. Among the members of the same species co-operation is so thoroughly carried out that it shames the efficiency of Knights errant during the Middle Ages.

But now let us turn to the fortunes of the human beings under the grip of the drought. The animals had no home nor luggage, so it was easy for them to emigrate in quest of food. But man, chained to his tilled field and tethered to his workshop, how could he effect a wholesale exodus? Who looked the most secure in normal circumstances was now most helpless under the weight of his many possessions and the blight of the heat. He could neither leave nor stay to see the ravages of the weather.

In six weeks some of our cattle looked like skeletons. Horses that raced before the heat set in, now languidly dragged their emaciated bodies from pasture to pasture looking for solitary blades of grass in a vast plain of sand and brown dead hard stubble. Every day the sun rose a ball of fire, and set like a burning disc of blood.

Human beings slowly ceased to be human. The fast-drying rill of the Avati had enough water for us to scoop up in cupfuls to fill the pitchers of the village. It took a long time to scoop up a few gallons of drinking water. As for washing—that was out of the question.

Our own farm was hardest hit, for it was farthest from the river and proved the most difficult to tend. So our cattle were let loose. They went wherever they pleased led all day by our bull, the strongest in the village. Our hired men ate at our table and shared our rice and curry once a day. For drink, each person was allowed two glasses of water—that was all. The most vivid impression of all here sank into my mind. If the animals of the jungle were acting in a compact well-disciplined army on the march, the civilised human beings were doing the contrary. After weeks of united effort which failed to drag our village out of its difficulties, each family began to act independently of its neighbours. This of course spelt disaster. For example, our cattle roamed in one direction, and that of our neighbours in another, and wild animals that happened to go by our village began to prey upon them. Had all the herdsmen let their cattle free in one place and stayed together, they could have raised the alarm and frightened the marauders away. But a lone herdsman, lying under a tree, could not frighten even a fox that had been hungry for weeks. It was a curious fact, the migrating beasts of prey rarely injured their untamed fellow fugitives, but whenever they met a cow, a horse or an ass tainted with the odour of domestication, they killed it without hesitation. The horror of the situation lay in the lack of alertness and initiative on the part of the domesticated beasts of burden. Used to the security of a village and accustomed to being guided and driven by man, they were not as capable and self-reliant as wild oxen or untamed nilgai. Their range of nose-sense, as we call it, was poor; they could not smell an approaching tiger within half the distance of that at which a common wild cow's nose could detect him. They were demoralised by civilisation; all their senses were dulled.

One day, I, instead of the hired man, took our cows to pasture about three miles down the river where there was a vast lake into which the river ran. We started about four in the morning in order to reach our destination before the heat of the day had become excessive. My slow-moving herd reached there not too late. The sun had already risen and set the entire countryside crackling with dryness. You could almost hear the earth's closed lips dried steadily by the sun's rays, till at last unable to bear that torture any more they cracked and opened. No human mouth could express so much agony. Those wide-open, terribly contorted lips of Mother Earth I shall not be able to erase from the tablets of my memory as long as I live. The signs of pain increased as we reached the lake shore. Alas, it was more shore than lake. In a weed-tangled baked cauldron of mud, about half a mile broad, lay a fathom of water a hundred yards in diameter. But thank the gods, despite what had been eaten by wild elephants and buffaloes on the march, there were plenty of lotus and lily stocks for the cattle. My cows fell upon them like locusts on a plentiful grain field.

About three in the afternoon we started homewards expecting to finish our journey in three hours.

A little before sundown the herd was stalked by a young panther. But only the big bull that led them knew it. Long before my wretched beasts I could perceive the panther's coming. I saw it as something continually kicking up dust back and forth on a parallel path about a couple of hundred feet away. The ground on which he was moving was so dusty that even a cat's footstep raised a screen of dust after it. The backward and forward drawing of that curtain of dust convinced me of his identity, for a man would only go in one direction and not back and forth on the same path. I drove my cattle toward him, for I was sure that within some yards of him their noses would scent the enemy. But their nostrils told them nothing, and seeing us coming, the panther vanished in the woods nearby, or perhaps he was crouching close to the ground. We went on and on and still there was no sign of any cat, and then the whole herd mooed and stopped together like one cow. At last they had sensed the odour of his presence and the whole herd was on him. Nevertheless he was so hungry that he leaped forward and charged. A flash of greenish gold rose in the air, turned black like a black pearl, and fell. . . . But my cattle were already running away. If they had only offered a united front! The leopard fell on the ground. In the rising dust I saw a darting ball of dull gold dash past me following the thundering of the fleeing hoofs, then I heard a yell, and that in turn was drowned by a groan.

It was my turn now to run, for I had to take advantage of the screen of dust ere it subsided, in order to get away from the vicinity of the angry panther. But hardly had I gone far when I heard a terrific bellow as if a dozen bulls were bellowing in unison, then a piercing yell of pain from the panther. More dust arose, blinding me and hiding the contestants from my sight. But I did not have long to wait, for past me dashed a raging bull, his flanks all blood and his head wreathed in red. With one more bellow of triumph he fell about a dozen yards from me. Again dust like a screen covered him from sight.

When that cloud had settled, I went forward to the leopard who lay dying, his garnet eyes imploring me to put him out of his misery. He had been ripped in two by the bull and slowly life ebbed out of his eyes. I turned back to the bull. His hump and neck and nose were torn. He had died instantly. Already flies, of whom very few had been seen in these days of drought, were swarming upon him from nowhere.

As I hastened homewards to find out what had happened to the rest of my cattle, I marvelled at the fury of our bull who had been ill-fed for days. I tried to think out what had happened. Our prize bull, the father of little Goma, must have faced the hungry panther in that cloud of dust, and because there was so much dust the panther had missed his aim. All the same, he had bitten and scratched fatally the neck-vein of the bull as the latter gored him with his horns and in desperation had clawed the air as he lay on his back, by chance ripping off the bull's nostrils.

Thinking in this fashion, I reached home and found that all the animals except one had got to the cowshed safely. Then I told my aunt what had happened, and in her joy of finding me at home safe and alive, she forgot to sorrow for the gallant bull who had given his body to save us all.

That evening I went with my aunt to a meeting of all the villagers at the temple under the guidance of Purohit. The entire community was stricken with panic. Famine and fires were predicted by every speaker. And since only rain, and at that very heavy rain, could avert a dire calamity, they urged the priest to order and organise a day of prayer and sacrifice.

My aunt said when came her turn to speak: "O, assembled civilised beings, do you not see that we are impure in our thoughts and speech? Do you not see that our minds are fear-stocked; our hearts heavy with suspicion, and our souls unanchored? Why are we thus rudderless and oarless? Because we have allowed ourselves to be afraid. I beg to request that we pray and fast as long as we are able to purify our thoughts and emotions and purge our beings of all dross. If we attain utter humility we are sure to pull down upon us the Infinite. Let us therefore be so humble that we may draw His blessings to us that the empty chalice may be filled." A pause followed. Apparently all the assembled civilised folk were of the same mind as my aunt.

At last the priest summed up the evening's discussion. "The water that is tranquil reflects the full moon. But if the wind blows in the night, the surface of the lake is cut and wrinkled and instead of one moon, men see in the water a thousand silver fragments, and know not whether they perceive a delusion or a truth. Like the pond is the human heart; if it be wrinkled with panic and seared with suspicion, it cannot render unto God the fulness of His Image when He looks into it. A soul's capacity to give limits its ability to receive. Therefore, O my brethren, go home and pray! Fast as long as you are able, but pray till the withering breath of devotion dries up the swamp of panic. Behold God in all things with the eye of your mind until God's compassion bursts forth out of it. Hari Om, tat sat Om!"

The congregation sat silently a while pondering the message of the priest, and then quietly walked home. The night was starry, but the sky was like polished steel, hard and merciless. Not a cloud anywhere—not even as small as the size of a humming bird. Kuri said to herself: "There is no least shadow of a sign that it may rain. The sky just does not know how to put on a cloud. My son, can you fast twenty-four hours."

I, who had not prepared myself for a quick answer repeated lamely, "Twenty-four hours?"

"Yes, each one must make a sacrifice," she replied. "The best sacrifice is to give up the pleasing of our appetites. No food, no drink, no fear, no woe! Your appetite and your mind will both be purified. Not to think of food, not to think of famine, but think of God's infinite benediction! Can you do that for twenty-four hours?"

I made no answer. This idea of fasting was not new to me, but to fast and pray steadily during one's waking hours was not easy. So I promised nothing to my aunt that night.

It was a terrible night. The hot wind blew fiercely making the temperature rise and still rise. Sleep was out of the question, and gradually the dust in the air grew so thick that everyone had to put a layer of cloth on eyes and mouth in order to save the lungs from being stuffed with inhaled dust. Kuri and I lay on our backs upon the roof watching the storm of wind and dirt. Seen through the layer of cloth on our eyes, and the whirling dust of the air, the stars shone like bits of red candle ends, all malice and cruelty. Like the angry eyes of a grim ogre, they watched us. During the small hours the wind rose to such a pitch that we had to run downstairs and take shelter in our rooms from the blown dust that stung our faces like needles.

Hardly had we barricaded ourselves behind our shut windows when we heard a terrific pounding against our front door. We went to it and tried hard to open it, but it was jammed. Again someone pounded loudly. It was uncanny. At last by dint of great pushing we succeeded in flinging it open and outwards which is the way all old Indian doors open. Before us a lanthorn in his hand, stood a man and instantly a fierce gust blew him into the house. All three of us pulled back the doors and barred them tight. What a tussle that proved to be! The man who had put down the lanthorn on the floor now unwound foot after foot of cloth from around his face and head. It was the priest! As if nothing strange had happened, he said quietly: "I have been to every household. Yours is the last. They are all praying in their homes. Will you too sit up and pray? I will join you."

We sat down in the vestibule around his burning lanthorn without any ceremony. Purohit gave us the theme of our devotion:

"Fear is not.
Suspicion is not.
Panic is not.

"O thou scimitar of courage come forth from within us and hew down the hills before us! Come forth, come forth, come forth! Pour, O rain! Blow, O wind! Come, O clouds, ye white bulls on your blue pasture! Peace and plenitude —Peace and plenitude—Peace and plenitude—Pour thy torrential compassion on all! Father and Mother of the Universe! Peace, peace, peace!"

Thus we meditated, while the wind raged outside with demoniacal wails. After daybreak the storm subsided. Men and animals emerged from homes and sheds. A new world greeted us. The earth seemed cleansed and swept, the sky, burning like a copper sheet, turned blue, yet looked unclouded by dust. We three human beings let the cattle do as they pleased and went off to the temple. Thither the other villagers were repairing to pray and fast. Since everybody knew the day's plan, the priest spoke little: "Many are praying at home. You assembled here pray also whole-heartedly—surely will the ear of Compassion Infinite be reached. I will smite the gong. Meditate before and after." He brought out of the inner shrine a large gong and smote it hard and long. The terrible clanging of the metal hammer on the metal disc was more unbearable than the raucous roar of the storm in the night. But it was necessary, for with every stroke of his hammer, he closed the senses of his congregation. Sound upon sound entered like corks of steel to stop the inflow into soul and mind of all impressions from without. This is the reason why the priests smite gongs and clang cymbals for half an hour sometimes, in the temples until their congregations are stilled enough for meditation.

There was another feature in the noise of this particular morning. The pitch of the hammering was intense, frequent and high. As though the sounds were not to float down sweetly like rills into the earth, they were driven and lashed upwards above the clouds into the very marrow of Heaven. That high shrieking flying procession of the cries of brass no God could resist, I thought! At last the priest stopped, and silence like a mantle was drawn over us all. The entire congregation was frozen into one solid mass of devotion.

It may seem incredible that when I opened my eyes the sun had risen to his zenith. I could not believe that I had prayed so long. I began to grow aware of myself—Can I explain to you what I mean? This was the first time in my life that I had been carried by the sincerity of my prayer so far that I felt no hunger, and, more surprising still, no thirst, of which all of us had been painfully aware ever since the drought had begun. My first sensation on regaining consciousness of the world was of the awareness of time. Then I looked around and saw the faces of men and women. With their eyes shut, they still sat lost in meditation.

Within the next thirty minutes, all of them came out of fathomless Silence. Each pair of eyes wore the glint of courage. We are cleansed and healed. The priest who had been meditating in the shrine came forward and spoke: "You have experienced a loss of self. Now that you are small God will be tall within you." He advised us: "Return home clad in humility. Observe silence all day. Do not speak of what you have felt and seen, for words destroy. Gather your cattle in your folds early this evening. Take all the necessary precautions for the coming cloudburst."

It seemed that whatever he said was heavy with truth. There was no mistaking his command. One by one the villagers walked home in silence. As Kuri and I were about to leave the priest detained her saying: "Will you permit the boy to spend the day here?" After nodding her head, which meant I could stay, my aunt went on her way alone. The priest said: "Pray with me as long as you are able, my son."

We prayed aloud for a while:

> "O father of the universe, give us rain!
> O mother of the universe, give us rain!
> Cleanse us of fear, suspicion and panic!
> Heal us of hate:
> Give us that which we need!
> As the one fire leaping out of many kinds of wood,
> As the one air that is breathed by all,
> As the one sun shining upon the world,
> Is untainted by the blemishes of what it shines upon;
> As the one Self
> Abiding in, yet unsullied by many selves;
> Come forth, O come forth;
> Cleanse, heal and sustain
> All thy sons—birds, beasts and men!"

This time it was difficult to plunge into prayer. The priest entered the inner world after a while, but I could not. I was too much tormented by the heat and too thirsty. I felt as if my tongue had swollen and had stuffed my mouth with cotton wool. I tried to meditate, but I said my prayer mechanically and without interest. After all, I was not yet fifteen years old: it was a harsh task that I had set myself to do, but there was no turning back. It was like meeting a tiger in the woods, it must be faced. But not quite yet—I opened my eyes and looked at the priest. He was far away from the realities of this world. Brow and eyes were calm as death, and his open palms on his lap lay like autumn leaves. When a man is lost in prayer like this, we say "he has lost his self," and rejoice, for unless this small self be forgotten or sacrificed, God's Self that is within us all cannot emerge.

I do not know how long I spent thinking in the above manner and studying the priest. At last something from within him seemed to come out and touch me; a feeling of gladness ran through me, and he opened his eyes. They were not eyes but caves of calm fire.

He said: "We will spend the rest of the afternoon singing to God." When we stopped it was nearly five. Both of us went out and looked at the sky. No sign of rain anywhere. "Now go home," said Purohit, "it is coming. The consecration that this village has created is bound to bring down God's compassion. There is no doubt in my mind."

About sundown a cloud arose in the south-eastern corner of the sky. About us the air became so still that even the few insects that had not died of the drought stopped chirping. Birds, such as crows and kites, ceased their flight. Cows and horses ran home from far distant pastures. The village dogs suddenly began to howl and whine. Men felt as if the tiny volume of air that they breathed would soon be taken away from them. With one more poignant yell the dogs ran away and hid. Stillness like a sucking vampire began to draw the very life out of the earth itself and one could feel it like a child pushing this invisible power with its helpless hands. Then rose a sudden groan as if it were strangling and a flash of lightning stung and curled around the cloud crest far away. Another groan—no, it was a long moan, then another period of stillness. Again that sucking away of all life . . . but not for long. Like the cheeping of a swarm of swifts came a clamour in the south-east, which changed into the drumming of a long rope on a distended sail, that, in turn, rose to the full-toned sound of vast wings beating the air. The people cried: "The storm, the storm!" As if awaiting this signal, the cloud rose and swept upwards growing larger and larger. Like black horses foaled by father sky the clouds flashed and flung forward. In ten more minutes dust, cloud and lightning, rolling, coiling, roaring, passed overhead and beyond to the Himalayas. Men and beasts shouted and bellowed thanksgiving as the first drops of rain reached at last the dying earth.

Time has gone by. Many years have passed. Even to this day when men say in my hearing that there is no power in prayer I answer: "If you beg always there is no power in prayer. But if you ask at the most terrible crisis not for yourself but for all the world, then surely your prayer, if it is attended with a sacrifice of self, will be answered by the Self of God."

A week after the coming of the rain the earth turned into a procession of leaping, shouting, burning torches of green. This is the power of prayer.

IX—Rathayatra or Juggernaut

IN India every occasion has its religious significance and symbolism. Now that the earth was green again and the rivers and brooks had reached their flood-tide, the ceremony of Rathayatra or Juggernaut and the attendant religious rites were held in every Hindu community.

Our own community trusted me, with other boys of the village, to go in the jungle in order to cut and fetch timber for the purpose of making a Rath, or chariot. But before I describe our jungle experiences, let me explain at the outset the nature and meaning of Rathayatra—Juggernaut.

It was the evening before our departure for the jungle that Purohit asked all of us to attend without fail the reading from the Shastras, the Scriptures. So along with most of the villagers many of the boys and myself went to hear him expound the meaning and symbolism of Rathayatra. After a short space of Silence, Purohit blessed us and then began.

"The festival of Rathayatra, the chariot of our Lord, that we shall observe a fortnight hence is as old as the seasons and as full of wisdom as a mine with gems. From time immemorial the Hindus have celebrated this festival. As you have heard before, it began with the Deluge. When our ancestors lived on the bank of the Indus river long before history learnt to stutter about man's existence, they were harried from time to time by the flooding of the Indus. Though young the race was full of wisdom, it read in the recurrence of the flood a challenge to men by the gods of Swarga (Olympus) whose chief was Indra.

"Since the One God, supreme over all gods and men, never took sides in the conflict of the two races, the human beings on earth devised the plan of fighting the gods under Indra, who were themselves little better than men. Mankind knew that the Supreme Being, Paramo Brahma, would not oppose the conquest of Indra and his celestials, so as soon as the latest deluge of the Indus had subsided, they set to build a tower of bricks that would withstand all the floods of all time. Slowly they laboured. They brought the silt from the river and made it into brick. They baked it till it became red and hard as stone, and when they had accumulated a mountain of bricks, higher it is said than the Himalayas, they set to erect their tower of safety. Brick on brick, tier upon tier rose the haughty structure. The gods, whose eyes are the stars, beheld it at each day's end and were perturbed. Indra told them that not only would the edifice withstand all their play with floods and deluge, the favourite pastime of the deities of Swarga, but that it was high enough to enable men to climb to its top and touch Heaven with mortal hands. That, all the gods agreed, could not be permitted. They pondered upon the ways and means of destroying the tower, and descending to earth and looking at it from every side, they perceived at last that one of its arches was not yet filled with bricks. This suggested to the chief, Indra, a malicious idea, and next morning when the men came to work, he, disguised as a man—a thing any god can do at any time—laboured with them. While at work he secretly placed false bricks—bricks that looked solid and red but were not of clay—into the empty arch. The mortals who could not see beyond the colour of the brick, applauded the craftsmanship and speed of this new man, never suspecting his disguise. At last when the building was done, the god slipped out at night and vanished into the sky where the other gods were waiting to congratulate him on his latest trick.

"Below on earth men rejoiced that night that their tower of security had been completed a month before the rain would fall. They feasted and bragged about their achievements all night long. Alas! poor mankind; they were not celebrating a triumph that night but magnifying their own stupidity.

"In time came the rain, and with it the rise of the

Indus. Higher and higher the water climbed, yet it could not break through the new-built tower. The flood groaned and rammed it like a thousand bulls, but in vain. Behind the building men were making ready to abandon the tilled fields and houses in order to take refuge on the tower. They were making towards it in a large boat when before their dazzled and puzzled eyes, the river licked up with its tongue the false bricks of red mud and made a hole in the tower, into which the river currents plunged like mad elephants, swirling, trumpeting and destroying. In a short time the tower was torn down and washed away, and the disastrous deluge carried everything —bricks, fields and houses in its teeth. It was fortunate that all the people were in their ark which however drifted helplessly on the waters that spun like black wheels of death. Seeing the success of Indra's trick played on mankind, the gods rejoiced in Swarga.

"From that time on, at the same season, men build a tower of wood everywhere in India to commemorate the meanness of the gods and to burn into the minds of our children the hope that some day they may build a structure to withstand pestilence, famine, and flood. O my brethren, the day is fast approaching when man will be secure against the malice of fortune and shall successfully meet the challenge of the gods." *

Here the priest stopped for breath. There was no doubt that though his audience had heard him many

* This is the Hindu account of the Deluge, Tower of Babel, and Noah's Ark. Did the writer of the Old Testament learn and write the story after the exile of the Jews in Babylon?

times before expound that scriptural account they were still visibly moved by his narration.

Purohit resumed. "You are touched, I behold, for you have passed through a harrowing siege of drought that threatened famine. Now that the earth is green and the rivers are all full again, let us build a tower, Rath, and place Juggernaut, Lord of the Universe, upon it. Every year we must build a tower and invoke God to stay in it eight days—to symbolize the duration of the eight weeks of flood. After that the deity should be placed in the temple here, and the tower, Rath, or chariot, will be broken up. During these eight days we must pray and live in moderation for they are days of hope for the future, when men shall no more fear flood or famine. Why (I perceive the question in your eyes) do we build a chariot instead of a tower of wood? Because it must be a structure which combines the tower and the ark in which our ancestors floated during the first deluge, and so we must build a moving building, a tower on wheels. . . . Now, O my brethren, let us bless these lads going into the woods to cut and fetch sandalwood for the consecrated building. May wild beasts never molest them, may the mercy of Heaven protect them, may our joint blessing guard and bring them back safely."

In previous years our village used the old chariot after repainting and repairing it, but this year because God had answered our prayers for rain, we planned to build a new chariot of sandalwood as a thank-offering. After the Rathayatra was over, the chariot would be broken up and each family of our community would receive a piece of it, its perpetual fragrance reminding them every day of God's mercy and love.

The three of us who went in quest of sandalwood were of various ages. Our leader, Samarth, was twenty, and I, fifteen, the youngest. We commandeered an elephant from a neighbouring Raja and set out for the jungle. The Raja was glad to lend his chief tusker for the purpose of serving religion. The Hathi (as an elephant is called in India) was about fifty years old. His back was spacious enough to accommodate a cargo of axes and ropes besides three human beings. We could trust our lives to the protection of his tusks which were thick and strong enough to guard a dozen lives. Samarth sat on his neck to act as Mahout, while I sat at the other end of the beast.

In six hours' time we had gone about fifty miles into the jungle, yet there was no sign of sandalwood. The forests were full of deodars (Indian cedar), ilex, cypress, pines, chestnuts and Himalayan oaks. Their leaves were new, and the colour of indigo. Parrots and parakeets flung their green sails in the sky as flock after flock flew up in the air at our approach. Wood-pigeons struck stentorian notes of warning to their fellows. And to the clamour of consternation of the frightened monkeys on the topmost boughs of a tree, a sleepy and irritated panther snarled a rebuke, almost a yard above our heads. We looked up. But at first no black cat could we find. We looked more carefully; lo, there lay a panther very far up a tree. Between him and us lay many long-spreading branches. His eyes glanced at us through a haze of sleep that made them burn like amber. After gazing at us steadily for a while, he shut them and went to sleep again. But we were not quite sure of that, since we could see him no more, for the elephant on which we sat had moved on silently. This we only became aware of by the chance touch of a passing branch, so softly did the sagacious creature move. He did not want the panther to know that we were running away from him. What wisdom lies in a Hathi's mind!

Let me assure you that I never forgot that panther. He was black as the shadow of the boughs under which he lay. Had it not been for his snarl and those desert-deep eyes, we should never have noticed him.

After eating our lunch at a brook side, we resumed our journey. We had to go very slowly for we were looking for sandal trees, and moreover since there was no road nor, track, we had to watch for branches of trees that might knock us off the Hathi's back. All that day we spent in vain looking for sandalwood.

At night we tethered the elephant's hindleg to a thick tree. We did so that his back might be amply protected. Between him and any attack from the rear lay the armour of a large oak tree, which we human beings soon climbed. We swung hammocks between its branches after examining all its arms and almost everyone of its leaves to make sure that no bird nested in it—which would have invited snakes who eat birds—nor was there on any portion of its bark the claw-mark of panther or any other kind of cat. Since some of us decided to stay up the night, we cut down small branches and made a machan (platform) between two parallel boughs close to the trunk. Then we all ate our supper and went up to rest. But there was no rest.

First the elephant below made a game for himself by flinging about our axes and crowbars which we had left on the ground. Insects started chirping, and waves of parakeets screamed as they flashed by in flocks; the call of the heron sounded far overhead, and about us papias dropped their exquisite trills. The song-sparrow struck his notes—only three; it was answered by another not far and that in turn by a third. Like needles of piercing beauty the notes fell . . . one, two, three. Then a pause. Now rose tia, tiata, tia, a, a—of the Doel, the Indian nightingale. With its far-reaching echoes the nest-dwellers fell asleep. Birds and beasts go to sleep at once. They do not thrash about in bed as human beings do, waiting and praying for slumber. The insects too had stopped their song below. Now silence was falling like jets of water, but not yet in an overwhelming stream. Two eagles sailed by. They cried at the sunset which had but passed. Then silence again, began to gush and run over the jungle, drawing after it sheets of darkness, till like black cotton wool, it lay in layers upon our eyes.

Nature is an artist of absolute taste. Into that risen pool of silence who would cast the first stone? A four-footed animal? No, that would be a sacrilege. A monkey's cry? No, that too would be banal.

Who should break the mirror of silence? Nature answered our question—it was the Doel's song tia tia la, a, a.

It fell like a handful of gold straws. The silence below and around was broken; it stole down and down into the roots of the earth.

Now came a soft crackling sound, followed by a snap. The elephant below had drawn in and put its trunk in its mouth. Snap, crack, snap, crack—came nearer and nearer. It almost touched our tree. The Hathi put his back against it; we felt the tree tremble. That instant with a short hard "Wao" the tiger bounded away from our vicinity. The elephant, we could feel, again unwound and brought out its trunk. But already many noises had begun afar off. Some buffaloes bellowed at the tiger's approach. Owls hooted. Wild boars grunted and dashed by. And away up in the sky, called by the nightingale, flocks of stars preened their silver wings.

About five in the morning we were roused from sleep by the shaking of our tree. We looked around, then down. One more shock and trembling of the tree! What was the matter with that elephant? There was not one but two. We rubbed our eyes and looked carefully. Lo, there were two elephants playing, trunk twined with trunk, walking backwards and forwards. And moreover our own elephant was untethered. The other one, apparently a wild young male, was playing with him. As the light of the day grew brighter, we could discern below that somehow the wild fellow had untied the rope from around his friend's feet. Having given him his freedom, he set to play with him, we inferred. But now we began to worry as to what would happen next. Would our Hathi run away with him, or what? Just then came the screech of parakeets and clamour of monkeys. We looked up. There, in a neighbouring tree, sat a flock of baboons, their arms outstretched to the east, shouting and singing to the rising sun. What an orison! It proved to my satisfaction our Purohit's teaching that animals worship their God as men do. The animals worship what they see—the sun. But men worship what they cannot see—God that dwells in every heart.

Hardly had the monkeys stopped when the two eagles came soaring by and circled as well as vaulted before the sun. Their clanging call blended with the miaowing of wild cats. Soon below us the wild elephant took leave of his tame friend and departed. In a moment he slid into the jungle like a black cloud in a deep dark sky—so silently and with such ease.

After our breakfast we packed and loaded our beast and set out for the teak forest, in whose depths the sandal trees grow. Fortunately it did not take us long to find it. By ten in the morning we were laying the axe to the roots of two trees. When they were half cut we tied hawsers around them, and made the elephant pull. The hawsers were long. Each time the tree fell far away from the elephant. We cut two more. Now began the hard part of our task. We had tied up the four trees, two on each side, then made the ropes fast around the elephant's neck, like the collar on a horse. At last we got on

A challenge to men by the gods
of Swarga whose chief was
Indra.

his back and started homeward. It took us four days to reach Mayavati. For the elephant had not only to pull and carry the load, but also had to find spacious tracks through which he could drag his train of lumber. How well he did it. Every few yards he would stop and look. Then he would put out his trunk to catch the scent of trees and empty spaces. From many odours he would choose the one from the desired direction and push towards it. It was marvelous to see him steer and tack. When we reached home, our families were glad to see us alive.

Now began the erecting of the Rath, the moving tower. The village carpenter came to take charge of the logs at the temple where he was asked to give the pledge that his soul and heart would be in the work and that he would pray and meditate most carefully while building it.

In a week's time the moving tower was ready, and the women of the village were set to decorating it with flower garlands, dyed silk, and leaves of trees. The wooden horses were painted by them, and the designs on the wheels in ochre and gold were wrought by the same hands. In the meantime, we, the boys of the community, had gathered flax and made strong thick ropes and tied them around the feet and the neck of the horses. Thus was all made ready.

On the auspicious day the priest brought out the god from the temple—the Juggernaut—Lord of the Universe, and placed it in the heart of the chariot. Then in the presence of the whole village he chanted:

"I call upon Thee
O Lord of the Universe
To gather all life
in Thine arms.
I call upon Thee to dwell
in this barge of a tower
While chaos and
clamour of waters
Rise flood upon flood
I pray in Thy Name to Thee
To preserve all in Thy compassionate Arms
Till the savage oxen of the tides stop roaring,
Till the charging black elephants of chaos subside.

* * * * *

Fling your voices O men and women
Like battle-flags before the procession,
Like the lances of thanksgiving,
While with mortal hands you pull the ropes
Tied to this house which treasures for eight days
The immortal God of the Universe.
Press on beyond death,
Press on beyond famine,
Press on beyond all suffering:
Battle beyond into the citadel of Life!"

At his words of command, boys and men pulled the ropes, and on moved the Rath of Juggernaut. We carried it to a temporary shelter at the end of the village, and we prayed and rejoiced for eight days. Plays were enacted on the temple grounds. Wrestling and fencing matches were held in the house of Palwan Lathiwal, while other contests such as running, jumping, Keet Keet, and Gooli Danda were staged on the fields. Even the cattle were given a holiday to do as they liked. The entire community acted as if there really had been a deluge, and they rejoiced as if they had been saved from real death. At the end of the eighth day the Rath of Juggernaut was brought back, the God was restored to the temple and the wooden structure given to the carpenter as a compensation for his labour.

* What Ghond describes takes place in every village of India. Even outside India in the Egypt of today, the Egyptians carry a symbolic ark from Luxor to Karnak. Thence after seven days it is brought back to Luxor amid feasts and rejoicing. Probably the experience of the Deluge is not only recorded in the Hindu and Jewish scriptures, but is a common heritage of all men.

X—Janma Stami, Or Celebrating the Birth of India's Christ

WITHIN a month of Rathayatra, the jungle had again grown thick and lush; no more wild animals came near the habitation of man. No more did we feel the stealthy eyes of panthers and tigers looking at our village, nor did we find anywhere the spoor of elephants. As if a play had been enacted and all its scenes removed, the green earth presented a new spectacle quite unimaginable to those who had seen it during the drought.

The grain-fields that had shot up like tricks of magic danced in the breeze by day and made small noises of growth at night. One could hear the corn thrust upwards one more inch with a soft explosive noise in the dark fields. Or if one listened, he heard the banana flowers open and let out the tender beginnings of their fruit. It surprised me to hear so many sounds at night. It led me to believe that even plants make noises of their own. Though I am an old man now and a hardened veteran of the jungle, yet I hold that the voices of saplings, grass, vines and trees, are probably the kindest and most delicate sounds that man has ever heard. I shall never forget one day when lying under a tree on the river bank, some strange noise softly drew my attention. It sounded as if a cow was licking her calf nearby. I looked all around—but found no one. So I put my face down into the grass and lay still. After what seemed a long while, I heard the same delicate yet firm sound of something soft brushing on a smooth but hard surface. Again failing to detect the source of it, I sat up and watched the water's edge whence the noise had come. There was no wind anywhere, and the river being full to the brim hardly made any sound. If one heard the water at all, it was almost imperceptible, like the yawn of a child. Just then the reeds before me shivered as if caught in a spasm. This hardly lasted a second, but the noise it made left no room for doubt as to its meaning. That entire day I neglected my duties and watched the reeds grow on the river bank and make that tender sound whose poignancy shall ever dwell in my heart.

Towards sundown I heard the temple trumpet sound—Honn—konko—n! That meant that Janmastami week had at last come and we must go to the temple and arrange for the Nativity of Our Lord.

At the temple, Purohit read from the Vishnu Purana an episode of the life of Krishna, and informed us that on the eighth night of the coming moon the drama of the Nativity of Krishna would be given and that we must prepare ourselves for it. The story he told us was the time-tested long miraculous tale of God's Incarnation, which a Hindu child can recite from memory from the age of ten on.

In India it is said that each temple celebrates at least thirteen religious festivals in twelve months. Our village and its place of worship was no exception to that rule. A temple should not only be a place of worship, it must combine the functions of the school and the theatre of the village. Nay, more than that; it must be the place where the needy receive charity and the sick are sometimes nursed. A house of worship should be open to all the experiences of Life.

The rainy season was not yet over. It went on raining till the morning of the Janmastami Day. Then the sky cleared and revealed a blue as intimate as one's own thoughts and as aloof as a haughty god. Such a tone of blue you never saw in your life; it was heavy as a blue rug and lighter than the air itself. There it hung—a mantle of magic.

The very hour of daybreak was like a scene in a theatre. Suddenly all the cattle, all the herdsmen and most of the villagers were found standing out of doors dressed and ready for the festivals. The cattle were let loose for the day. Then the herdsmen brought fruits and flowers from their respective houses and offered them to the temple. Now came a procession of girls of every household, their dresses gleaming as waters of gold and their feet raising a silver din of bells and anklets. When they stood before the shrine and put down their little gifts and bowed to the priest, he blessed them thus:

> "May you so live that one day you may become
> the mother of God's next Incarnation on earth. 2
> God may be born without a human father, but a human mother He must have. *You mothers of men and women, you daughters of men and women, may you be the mothers of the Avataras (the next Divine Incarnation).*"

All day people came and received their blessings from the priest, during which time the majority of us fasted. At last, when the sunset approached, the priest again recited the Nativity story from the scriptures. Then he blessed the rice and the sweetmeats that had been offered at the temple by the whole village. After his blessings, these articles of diet attained a spiritual significance.* They were liturgic now—those who betook of them became

* It is the same thing when the Christians take the Communion bread and wine. Apparently other races practise a similar ritual.

brothers. After it, bells were rung; gongs groaned; and conch shells were blown. All of us rejoiced since God was born amongst us in our spirit. We were all brothers and sisters now.

But we, the boys and girls of the village, had no time to amuse ourselves, for the task of performing the play of the Nativity was entrusted to us by the community. I was the Prologue. I had to explain the nature and meaning and the necessity of the play, before the play began. So I went off into a corner and kept repeating to myself my lines. I always forgot some words. Mine was also the duty to invoke solemnity:

> "Now that you are here, may contemplation and deep thought come forth from you."

Can you imagine a boy of fourteen saying to people of forty: "May you learn to think!" Thus while I was worrying myself about acting my part competently, the torches had been lighted, old rugs had been placed on the temple ground, and the entire audience had stopped rejoicing and taken its seat.

Our audience sat on rugs occupying most of the space save a circle of about twenty feet in the centre. From that spot ran out a path about a foot wide all the way through the audience far out into the basement of the temple where the green-rooms were located and the actors were putting on their masks. With the exception of myself, almost all of the characters either wore masks or painted their faces. Since it was a miracle play of great religious import, no actor must wear a merely human appearance. He must have something, some mark or mask on his face to convey to the audience that he was twofold—as all human beings are—both human and divine.* Even grotesque masks were used in order to achieve that end.

At last three musicians, two vehala-players, violinists, and the beater of drums, walked through the audience into the circle and played a tune. At the end of it, I walked to the centre of the stage and beat together two cymbals—clang, bang, clang! Then with shaking knees, trembling tongue, and a battering ram of a heart within me, I began:

"O assembled civilised beings!" Here my tongue clicked in my mouth like the wooden clapper of a cowbell. Someone in the audience murmured "He needs a drink." This remark enraged me so that I pulled my tongue as a horseman pulls his reins and brings his wayward animal to its senses. I shouted again: "O assembled civilised beings," as if their being civilised could help me. Strangely enough, it did. Those words made my tongue move as I wished.

"From time immemorial," I resumed, "our religion has insisted that whenever virtue is in decadence and vice is in the ascendance, God incarnates in human form to conquer the latter and to release virtue and righteousness from their dungeon. In our hearts virtue is in chains and vice roams free as a leopard in the jungle. It slays the kine, our good impulses; it devours the sheep, our gentle spirit. It

* What Ghond says of actors in a religious play applies to Hindu works of sculpture: each sculptor hews stones into human figures, yet twists them so that they look superhuman.

is untamed, untrammeled and ever-rebellious. It must be slain if good is to flourish within us, and if God is to reign in all! Therefore, watch this play. Listen to its simple but solemn words! Whip up the charger of your concentration; follow each flying word till you trap and make its meaning your own.

"O civilised assembled beings, crane the neck of your attention, bend your soul's hearing, attend and gather from my feeble lips the history of Our Lord's Nativity that took place in bygone times.

"In the days of yore He incarnated many times to bring about the triumph of Righteousness. He has been born in other races and other climates. He may in the future be born a man or a woman. There is no last nor first incarnation of God, says our religion, and all religions lead to the same God.

"Tonight we are in Magadha, the capital of the wicked King Kangsa. He is so vicious that God is troubled by his misdeeds. All humanity prays to God to deliver the world from Kangsa. But God cannot be born save in the heart of a pure woman, a woman who will not sin. So, leaning on the parapet of Heaven, God looks searchingly for a sinless soul. Lo, he finds in the king's sister Devaki the purest mother, and instantly God incarnates on earth. A prophecy is heard in the king's court: 'O thou sword of sin, thou hammer of vice, thou spear of death; he who will destroy thee and save the world from ruin is to be one of the eight sons of thy sister. Beware! And sin no more.'

"But this, instead of checking Kangsa from committing more sins, spurs him on. He at once sends out an army and arrests his sister Devaki and her husband Basudeva, and flings them into a dungeon ten fathoms deep underground. There eight months pass." Now I smote my cymbals together and the violinists who were accompanying my speech stopped playing. It was over. I crept away from the centre of the stage and joined the audience. Through the little lane came from the green-rooms Basudeva and Devaki in captives' chains, groaning under the strokes of the prison warden's rod. He was brandishing a ten foot bamboo pole behind them and yelling like a wounded beast. Though in pain, neither of the prisoners showed any signs of anger or indignation. They were resigned to the will of Heaven. The queen was weary and spent by the effort of carrying God under her heart and bearing the persecution of the world. Now that they had come on the stage the warden said: "God be thanked that your walk in the fresh air is over; you are the only prisoners allowed such a privilege. It upsets all our prison routine to have to see to it that you get your day's exercise. For the bother that you have caused me take that, and that." After hitting them again, he left the stage growling like a beast and shaking his mask of a tiger's head at everybody.

Basudeva and the mother of God, who had not complained at all, now held a discourse.

Mother of God said, "Seven of my children have been slain by the order of the wicked king, my brother, O God, why did you choose me to be your mother? You know not how frail my heart is."

Basudeva: "Let us not sorrow for the lost. It is

the eighth one that we must think of—how shall we save him from the devouring monster, your brother? How, O God, can we give the world your coming Incarnation? Show us the way, O beneficent washer-away of all sorrow."

In answer to their prayer at once appeared in the gaol a celestial being with wings and golden vestments.

"O Basudeva, the Child will be born tonight. There is rain abroad and the river is in flood. As soon as the Child is born, bear him on your back across the flood screened by the rain, to the village of Gokul where the herdsmen live. The herdsmen's chief is called Nanda. Nanda's wife has given birth to a child. This babe is but an immortal spirit. Leave your son at the queen's side. She will not know the change, for the two babes look alike. One of God's celestial attendants has gone ahead and left all the doors and windows unbolted at Nanda's palace across the river in Gokul."

With these words the divine messenger vanished. Basudeva looked round, and to his amazement he found that there was no one there but that someone had untied his hands. At that moment King Kangsa came on the stage. Basudeva held his own hands behind his back as if they were still tied together.

"How well you look, my sister," said the wicked king through his fiend's mask. "And you, too, brother-in-law. I have come to see you in secret. For it is not pleasant to be followed by my royal servitors every moment, especially when the task is so delicate; my sister, evil omens befall me wherever I go. The astrologer royal who casts horoscopes and who reads my fortune every day, tells me that you are expecting your eighth son tonight, and I must take every precaution and strangle it the moment it is born. Since my servants are bored by killing your children, I have decided to throttle the next one myself. Come, therefore, to the royal palace and abide with my women where I may keep an eye on you. It is unkingly for me to be here."

At this, his sister fell on her knees and begged him to let her next child live. "Spare one, only one to me, O my noble brother. You have destroyed seven, but spare one."

But Kangsa is hard as whetted steel, and leads them away to a special dungeon in another place.

At the end of the act, the musicians played a deep-toned sad composition at the finish of which I got up and said after clanging my cymbals:

"Rejoice, the divine Child is born. The tyrant cannot kill him. He will reach safety in Gokul and thrive like the waxing moon among the herdsmen."

While I was saying my lines Devaki and Basudeva had stealthily filtered through the audience with a child and were sitting on the stage. As I sat down, they rose and caught the eye of the people. Devaki held the child in her arms while Basudeva put his hand to his ear and listened. "It rains as if the very universe were being washed away." He goes forward and examines the lane through the audience, and goes off towards the green-room. But he returns. "Hasten, beloved. Give me the child. The sentries sleep. Your brother, too, sleeps. None has heard the child cry. I must take it across the flood before the keepers of our dungeon awake."

"How can I part with it, my Lord?"

"Part with it you must, dear wife, for its life hangs on a thread."

"Let me behold its sun-shaming countenance once again. Once more. Nay, once more if you please."

But no more. Devaki cried out: "God, I pray Thee not to burden another woman with the terrible task of bearing Thee under her heart." With these words she retired into the audience.

Now came Basudeva with the Divine Child. He said: "The flood is too high. The current is strong enough to fell a tree. How may I cross it? O Ruler of the universe, give me strength to carry Thee across. O my Master, strengthen my arms give me guidance! I beg Thee, O compassionate One, to show me the way."

Again his prayer was answered. A jackal came from nowhere and crossed the stage, making noises.

"Ha!" says Basudeva. "Another sign! On, on, my poor legs! On across to Gokul to the home of the herdsmen. O God, Thou friend of the oppressed, uplifter of the downtrodden and the leader of the righteous, make me true and strong at this moment. Give me the power to love justice and conquer wrong."

With these words he plunged into the water and laboriously waded across the flood. He arrived at the other side, and the audience applauded in a frenzy of joy, shouting: "God is born in our midst. God has come to earth again."

Now the priest of the temple strode forward and pronounced his blessings. "The midnight hour is nigh. The stars are silent in awe before the spectacle that we have seen. You all know how, when he learned of Krishna's escape in Basudeva's arms, the wicked king ordered a massacre of all children. But he was not given power to hurt the Divine Child—with the sun-shaming face of compassion.

"God is reborn in our hearts tonight. May we keep Him alive in our inmost selves. Go home in silence. Do not fritter away the meaning and message of this play in talk. Silence and meditation—may they guard and consecrate the days that are before you, *Hari Om, Shanti Om!*" *

* The story of Krishna's Nativity bears a great resemblance to that of Jesus. St. Christopher carried the Christ child across the flood. After the birth of Jesus there was a massacre of the innocents. In their later years, Jesus and Krishna did many similar miracles. It is interesting to bear in mind that no one yet knows how the two histories came to resemble each other.

XI—New Experiences

My fifteenth year was the most interesting year of my boyhood. But of its most important event I will tell you later: here let me describe one of our curious institutions, that of "Dharna" prevalent in India forty years ago. Dharna is a system that has come down from ancient times when men lent money to one another without documents or witnesses. You may imagine how hard it was to collect the debts! There was no way of making a debtor pay unless he wished to, so the creditor had to resort to very strange means.

Our nearest neighbour in Mayavati was Kalu the grocer. He was fat as an ox and ugly as a weasel. He made money out of whatever he touched, but the more money he had the meaner he became. He borrowed money from everybody and paid it back only after a great deal of moral persuasion and pressure. This money that he borrowed he used in all kinds of successful speculations. For instance, during the drought he persuaded Purohit, the priest, though a poor man, to lend him all he had, three hundred rupees,* and speculated with it in grain and fodder.

After the Rathayatra of Juggernaut and the Janmastami festivals, the priest went to Kalu and asked him for the return of his funds. But Kalu stared out of his fat face saying: "You are mistaken, I owe you no money."

Purohit replied: "Let me refresh your busy mind, which seems to cultivate the art of forgetfulness to such perfection! Last May after the New Year † when the drought was at its height, and the old year with its agony had come to its end, you borrowed three hundred rupees in the dark under the Banyan tree of the village threshing floor!"

Kalu pursed his lips thick as a mat and said: "Let me look into my book. My memory is poor. All the

* One hundred dollars.

† The Hindu year begins about the fifteenth of May, just when the drought ends and the rain begins.

business I transact I put down in my book. . . . Lo, there is no entry of any sort after the 1st of Baisakh, the first month of the year!" *

This so enraged Purohit that he threatened Dharna. "If you do not bring me my money by sundown today, from tomorrow morning I shall sit by your front door and fast continually until you discharge to me your lawful debt. Tomorrow at seven in the morning I will begin Dharna, unless you cudgel your poor memory and recall your indebtedness."

Kalu did not cudgel his memory; he would recall no indebtedness that involved giving up three hundred precious rupees.

Punctually at seven the next morning, Purohit came to Kalu's door and uttered a short prayer: "May I suffer so that it will purify me! May my pain be so pure that it will remove the stone that is blocking the entrance to brother Kalu's memory. Peace and love to all!"

He sat there and fasted the whole day but nothing happened. Kalu went on buying and selling at his shop as if there were no priest within sight or hearing.

The next day the priest came again and performed Dharna. But Kalu paid no attention to him. The priest handed over the business of the temple to another Brahmin from a neighbouring village, in order to fast day and night without interruption at Kalu's door. This dissipated all doubts from every

* The Hindu year begins about the fifteenth of May, just when the drought ends and the rain begins.

mind that Kalu owed money to Purohit for no one, most of the villagers reasoned, who had not lent money would go to the trouble of fasting like that.

The priest, whose duty consisted in promoting a man's spiritual evolution, desired not only to recover his wealth but to save the grocer's soul, which this sin would put far back on its way to God. He felt he must sit out his Dharna even if it killed him.

A fortnight passed, but Kalu was unmoved. Purohit grew so thin he had to be carried to his martyrdom on a cot.

Now the whole village took sides; one-third for Kalu and the rest for the priest. The former insisted that Kalu was telling the truth, and that the priest, being an unpractical man was talking nonsense, for none dared accuse Purohit of deliberate mendacity. The friends of Purohit would like to have boycotted Kalu but this was impossible for he was the only grocer and money changer we had and so, as there was no way of bringing him to his senses, the contest went on. Purohit fasted about ten days more.

But on the 25th day in the forenoon the "Singa," the temple trumpet, was sounded. All who could leave work and as many boys as could obtain permission, ran to the temple. As we went we found the grocer's shop closed and no priest fasting nearby, which whetted our curiosity so much that we ran all the faster. We reached the upper floor of the temple, and there in the presence of nearly the whole village, beheld Kalu squatting on the temple floor with beads of tears running down his fat wrinkled cheeks in runnels. Being a versatile fellow he wept and spoke at the same time:

"O brethren, how can I tell you of the marvelous dream that I have had? God Himself in the form of a shepherd came to my bedside last night and pulled me by the hand. I arose, in my sleep, all unconscious, and followed where He led me. My Divine Mentor took me downstairs to my cash-room where my account books are kept and there pointed out a book. Wonder of wonders! No light was burning, yet I could see and read in it. I turned the pages that He wished me to turn, until, lo and behold, there under the priest's name, lay an entry of three hundred rupees! The book fell from my hand. I bent down for it and when I stood up and looked my companion was gone. This aroused me from sleep. Was I surprised to find myself on my feet instead of in my bed? No, but I was startled to find this account book of last year open at this entry, just as it was in my dream. Look and see for yourselves—see the priest's name, and sinner that I am, I have come to beg forgiveness not only from Purohit but from you, my brothers and sisters. Say you forgive me!"

We all looked at the previous year's account book and saw on the last page but one the entry in Kalu's hand. He sat before us shedding cataracts of tears. There was nothing to do but forgive his sin and rejoice. The starving priest who had been carried in a cot to and from Kalu's front door for the last three weeks was now brought upstairs. He raised a feeble hand in the gesture of forgiveness which moved Kalu so that he buried his face in his arms. Someone brought a glass of mango juice with which the priest broke his fast of Dharna.

Even now you will find a creditor sitting Dharna at the door of his debtor in those parts of India where pests such as laws and lawyers are still uncommon. Not only in collecting debts but in many other things the Hindu victims practise similar penances in order to awaken in the wrong-doer's soul the consciousness of his guilt. It is most efficacious if carried on without hate, envy, and avarice.

XII—We Visit Agra, Delhi and Kashmere

By the end of August my aunt and I travelled beyond the British territory to Jammu, north-west of Kashmere, in order to inspect our property. There we had our ancient home, a few acres of pasture land. For seven hundred years our ancestors had lived there. The house that they had built from which our family had migrated only recently had stood intact for centuries. Hindus have such respect for their ancestors that they will not abandon their ancient homestead, and it is considered spiritually beneficial to revisit the birthplace of one's forefathers now and then. The distance from Mayavati being great and the journey most arduous, my aunt went to Jammu only once in five years. This year she decided to take me with her for she was getting old and besides she wanted to show our tenants the face of her successor.

I, who had never been to Kashmere or Jammu, was only too delighted to go. We journeyed on foot below Almora where we entrained for Allahabad. Allahabad is a Mohammedan name; it means Allahka "bad," the abode or city of God. It is also a sacred city of the Hindus, for here the sacred rivers, the Ganges and Jumna meet. Every thirteen years about ten million Hindus make a pilgrimage to Allahabad in order to bathe in the confluence of the two streams.

From Allahabad we went by train to Agra. There we spent two days at the Taj Mahal, the mausoleum of Mam Taj Mahal. Who has not heard of that gem of architecture, matchless in all the world? Shall I ever forget its marble majesty? Can I ever erase from my soul its exquisite and eternal sadness? The human race should be divided into two classes: namely those who have seen the Taj Mahal and those who have not.

It is surrounded by a green garden inside high red sandstone enclosures. You come along a dusty road that ends alongside that red wall, which hides everything from the view save the sky that rests on it like the emerald arm of a god. After going along the wall you come upon a very tall gateway turreted and ornamented like the back of an elephant covered with domes of cornelian. As you stand in the gateway you see the green-black cypresses; from the deep red sandstone to such green is a moving surprise. But look beyond: like a thousand coveys of milk-white doves rises the dome of the Taj Mahal. Before it half a mile of fountains are sobbing in the gathering evening dusk. Music and magic pierce your eyes and ears. The sorrow that a king consecrated in the hard marble has become the song of all ages. What you see as you draw nearer the vast mausoleum is nothing compared with what you cannot see. The invisible presses upon you through every fold and texture of the visible.

Now as you stand close to it, you realise how high it soars above this world, yet its roots are buried in the soil of our everyday life. You look down, it becomes as intimate as the face of your beloved; when you look up, an exquisite ache grips your heart, for you fear that such an unearthly vision is bound to fly away any moment to the skies whence it came. The wonder of untainted whiteness shivers, as breath upon breath of awakening colours broider its edges. Like the trembling of the wings of a dragonfly, delicate and intensely clear tones hover over the entire edifice. The fountains stop their sobbing. The last notes of a bird die in the distance. Nothing stirs. Lo, now the Taj wrapped in vestures of glimmering silence sits on the throne of night. All this colour glowing like the cheek of a bride, whence comes it? Is it the risen moon that has lifted the white veil of death and revealed to your startled eyes the face of your love—Mam Taj Mahal? Hour after hour her presence works its enchantment on you. She is no more dead. She responds to you as if you had touched her hand. Suddenly rushes upon you the realisation that Immortality has torn and thrown away the veil of death, and thrust upon you its terrible splendour. What you see now is no more a speechless stone, for it is tongued with Truth.

"Yea, I shall live if you remember," you hear the marble say to you, as spoke the empress Mam Taj Mahal to her distracted husband while she lay on her death-bed more than three hundred years ago. You can also hear his answer coming out of your own throat, "Yea, the whole world will remember."

No sooner had Emperor Sha Jehan spoken those words than her body released her heaven-hungry soul. Then he too was stricken by a fell disease and from that time on, he lay in his invalid's bed in the Jasmine Tower and dreamt how best to preserve her memory. Not only he, her husband, but also the whole world, needed a perfect chalice to hold the beauty of her face.

After six years of meditation in the Jasmine Tower he saw in a vision the turrets and the dome of the Taj Mahal. In order not to lose any time, he smote the silver gong that hung by his bedside. Attendants rushed to answer his call. "Send for all the architects of the world. I have found it, I have found it. Naksa, naksa! Bring me parchment and ink, let me copy it ere it steals out of my memory."

He drew day and night while architects gathered around him and watched him make the plan of the mausoleum. Their eyes marvelled at the vision while it rose black line by black line, curve on curve as the emperor's pen coursed on the white parchment. Their hearts quailed at the thought of the time and wealth the building would cost. But the emperor was adamant.

"Fourteen years and seventeen thousand men at work every day, say you! So shall it be. Empty the coffers of the state, plunder my private treasury. But build! Let workmen come from India, China, Persia, Egypt, Ceylon, Italy, nay, invite the whole world to consecrate my dream."

Not only foreign workmen came with their tools but the Indians themselves went out in flocks to fetch the precious stones necessary for the work of the mosaic. They crossed the Himalayas to China for jade, green as the eyes of spring; and penetrated with caravans into the Egyptian desert for the perfect cat's-eyes. They disembowelled half of Burma for rubies, and exhausted Damascus of its amber beads. Lapis and onyx came from Italy; while agate, garnet and moonstones streamed from the confines of the southern seas.

Though he was terribly ill, Shah Jehan never surrendered. He lived on by the strength of his purpose, month by month, year by year, till the structure rose and fulfilled his dream. The day the empress was buried under it, he lay in his all too familiar bed of illness and heard the cannon boom its last and final salute to the interment of the Mam Taj. Then he said: "I come, beloved, I come—to lie beside you." Alas, death that had taken her would not take him when he wished. For a few years he lingered more dead than alive, but at last when his time came he was buried next to her.

I would any time rather give up my adventures

in the jungle than give up my first vision of the Taj that moonlit evening forty-five years ago. With the javelin of beauty still piercing our heart, we wended our way home eager to leave Agra on the morrow for Delhi and Jammu. How can any man revisit or reiterate such experience!

Next day on the train Kuri and I spoke not a word. Though we reached Delhi in a short time, instead of seeing the works of art there, we went to the river bank and loitered all day.

The word Delhi should be pronounced Dilli or ravisher of hearts; better still, the heart itself. Agra was important because it had the Taj. But Delhi was important in quite a different sense. Its grandeur lay in the city itself. No matter where you turned, your feet trod upon the past. Thousands of years ago, Hindu emperors ruled it and called it Hastinpore or Elephant city. Here assembled the largest number of elephants of India, for hither they brought on their backs hundreds of the chiefs and vassals of the Hindu's emperors to do homage to their master. Later on when the Indian Mohammedan rulers built their capital, they called it The Heart. And it is a city that gladdens a boy's heart. Here you see a magician who makes trees grow on the road. He puts a man in a basket, then lo, there is nothing in the receptacle! He makes a man go up a rope, the man and rope both vanish into the nothingness of the sky. Dilli—ravisher of a boy's heart indeed! What a city!

Then there is the circus. A man puts his head in a tiger's mouth, does the tiger chew it as a cow would chew a raw potato? Wonder upon wonder: he withdraws his head unharmed! Now he makes one of three tigers stand on his hindlegs and walk like a dog. Then something happens very quickly, one of the other tigers tears at him from behind. He faces it with lightning agility, and so lashes it with his whip till it becomes quiet. But the performance is spoiled. He is perspiring profusely as he comes out of the cage. While the audience is applauding him, I ask my aunt to take me to the green-room where I can see the man. He had fired my imagination with his performance, but he had roused my worst apprehensions as well. Kuri acceded to my request. When we found the green-rooms we were told that the tiger tamer was walking outside in the open, under the stars, so we hastened thither. Since he had his uniform on and gave out a strange odour—odour of tiger and fear combined—we identified him soon. He lay on the grass an utterly spent man. He did not even notice our approach.

My aunt spoke first. "Sir, please excuse our intruding on you. My child is so tormented by eagerness and admiration that he insists on speaking to you."

After signing to us to sit down, the man sat up and squatted on the grass. "I am glad that someone wishes to hear me and speak to me. I am a wretched man. I wonder if I shall outlive another week's performance."

"Indeed!"

"Yea, the beasts have outwitted my vigilance twice

Fourteen years and seventeen thousand men at work every day, say you! So shall it be.

in three days. I do not know what is the matter with me."

I made bold and answered: "You are frightened. They smell fear which your body gives out. You perspire fear."

"Ha, what fairy tale is this? Dost thou speak wisdom to one who has lived amongst animals and tamed them all his life?" he taunted me.

"Nay, sir, I speak no wisdom, but I smelt the fear myself which your body exuded. I was very close to the cage in which you performed."

"Indeed!" he ejaculated again with sarcasm. "I am a Santal of the central province. I need learn nothing about animals from you. Dost thou know that the children of our tribe milk wolf mothers as if they were goats?"

"All the same, sir," I insisted, "if I were you I would smear my body with castor oil the next time I go into that cage. It will take some time to conquer your fear. You will have to purge your mind slowly with prayers. Until that happens, you had better cover the odour of fear with an odour that those tigers will find utterly foreign and inexplicable to their nostrils. That will baffle them!"

"Thank you, I will do no such thing," he said in anger.

"Farewell, sir, I have spoken what the gods within me clamoured to express." Without bandying any further words with him we left, expecting not to see him again alive on this earth.

The next day we spent in visiting the works of art

in Delhi. Though none has as noble a history as the Taj yet some of them are as unique as that exquisite mausoleum at Agra. The Moti or Pear Mosque is the purest temple of worship that I have seen. It was built by Shah Jehan's son, Aurangzeb. The latter was a Mohammedan bigot of the worst type. He never dared to build anything that did not enhance the prestige of Mohammedanism. He hated his father's love of beauty that was divorced from religion, so he built to celebrate the powers of Islam. All the same that mosque called Moti is exquisite as the hollow of a pearl.* It stands inside the Dewani Khash and Dewani Am, those two royal reception halls that Shah Jehan built. Both the Am and the Khash (inner and outer reception chambers) are marble pavilions whose arcade is full of nine-pointed arches, and whose marble pillars and ceilings wear magnificent mosaics of onyx and lapis lazuli, designed as flowers and foliage within, and curving of blades of chalcedony outside. And the utter restlessness of the design finds perfect rest in the harmony that all the colours, curves and points make when seen as a whole.

There in a fabulous tropical garden bower of marble and semi-precious stones stood the peacock throne, a wizardry of gold and emerald, topaz and sapphire. And there only two hundred years ago sat enthroned the great Mogul with the largest diamond of the world, the Kohinoor, shining from his crown. Now, though that most precious throne is stolen and

* Ghond is wrong. Moti Masjid was built by Shah Jehan himself according to most historians.

taken to a foreign land, and that diamond, too, the foreigner has taken far away from India, the Dewani Khash and the Am still remain cooled by rushing water that has been running under them ever since Emperor Shah Jehan built them.

And if you wish to dream, you may sit there and conjure up the splendours which even now are more sumptuous than anything that stands intact in all Northern India.

Delhi also has a mosque built by Shah Jehan, a little over three hundred years ago. It is the Jumma or Friday Masjid, House of Worship. It is of thick slabs of red sandstone inlaid with large leaves of gold, a place of worship fit for emperors. The walls are thick as two elephants, and the arches are so numerous that one wonders that they were ever carved.

Every Friday afternoon when the muezzin calls people to pray there, one feels like saying: "All prayer is superfluous, brethren, in this house which itself is the most sumptuous gesture of a prayer."

The only thing that can surpass the Delhi of the Moguls is the old Delhi seven miles away from Jumma Masjid. How destroyed beauty surpasses living splendour we felt to the full when we went to the old Delhi the next day.

It lay ruin upon ruin. Hindu palaces of ancient times were buried under the temple of Prithviraf of the Middle Ages. That in turn lay under the Mohammedan structures of the 13th and 15th centuries. They were all enclosed by a thick red wall pierced with tall arches. Among the destruction and the decay of the old Delhi stood one living splendour, floating like a banner to the sky. It is the commemoration steel pillar of the ancient Hindu kings, a pillar of strange combination of copper and steel full of inscriptions which glisten without any sign of decay. It has been standing in the open for two thousand years and has not rusted yet.* It quickened my boyish imagination to think that the ancient Hindus were masters of a secret that cannot be found out.

After that steel column, what put ecstasy into my soul most powerfully was the vision of the burning blue sky caparisoning many miles of red sandstone broken here and there by shells hurled by the Hindus and the English during the war of 1857. As we trod on yellow and white ruins and went along that wall, suddenly we came to the foot of a very high arch. Where we stood we could not see its top, so we moved away walking backwards. Then as the red arms rose higher and higher and the top drew downward into view, lo, instead of meeting each other—they remained apart. The top was broken. And between those scarlet shoulders, instead of a point of sunlit red, the vibrant blue sky thrust itself like the breast of a peacock. The surprise of colour and the shock of beauty was so great that I shut my eyes for a moment. Ever since, I have remained a slave of the ruins of ancient India, whether they be Fatehpoor Sikri, that waste of sandstone and

* Like the art of mummifying the dead in Egypt, the Hindu art of creating rustless steel is dead and gone. Though many clever people have cut pieces off that metal pillar and sought for its secret by studying them, yet the wizardry of the old coppersmiths eludes them still.

marble, or the deserted city of Amber, a garden of granite where tigers wander and yell and the eagles screech at noon. Ah, those old, old cities! Their broken walls are as broken bread and their torn roads are precious ancient shawls. Food and clothing they are to the spirit of Man!

From Delhi we went to Jodhpore. It is a city of many colours. Seen at sundown from the hillside behind it, Jodhpore spreads like a cloth of gold inwrought with ruby, lapis lazuli, topaz and cornelian. Camels with their supercilious gaze thread the streets in silence, while elephants caparisoned in saffron ring their silver bells hanging from silver chains. Suddenly a solemn and uncanny feeling seizes one. It is the effect of the city sounds on one's hearing. The builders of Jodhpore in order to amuse their king, built it so that if the royal ruler stood on this hillside, he would hear most distinctly each and all of the noises of his city. It is unearthly for a man to hear so clearly and powerfully so many things coming up from far below. Sound after sound we heard: the camels' hushed tread, the elephants' bells, the hoofs of the horses, the cry of the vendors, the yells of the street urchins, women's thin voices from different housetops, men bargaining in the mart, and above all the tolling of the temple bells announcing the hour of silence—all came swarming up, beating their wings on the dumb rocks like the supplications of a thousand souls before their long dead deity.

After the hillside of Jodhpore we went to Rawal Pindi, under which lay ancient Taxila, another ruined and buried city. Thence by caravan we went to Srinagar, the capital of Kashmere. There we rented boathouses and set out on Lake Dal. Boathouses are strange things. Imagine yourself in a house floating up and down the lake, rowed hither and thither by eight boatmen bare to the waist, their muscles strained in statue-like grace. Thus we went day after day along the purple side of the Himalayas, drawing behind us our silver train of murmuring water.

The Indian labourers, no matter what the nature of their work, had one thing in common, their habit of singing. Toil without song was unknown in my youth. In Kashmere as elsewhere the boatmen sang while they rowed. It was so pleasant to hear the water make its cool sounds against the side of our floating house in between pauses of boat music.

As yet the snows of the Himalayas were invisible, but the thick green forests of the hills frowned at us every dawn from their haughty heights. Birds innumerable flew overhead from early twilight till the gathering purple gloom of eventide. Flocks of swallows twittered and flung their patterned shadows like shawls on the white waters. Geese, those wise ungainly caravaners, thrust their clear keen wedge into the horizon; white eagles made their rare appearance, stilling even the jumping of the fish on the water, and far away from where they plunged, storks stood on the water's edge meditating on the nature of food.

Now that autumn was at hand migration characterised the life of almost all the animals.

In seven more days we reached our home. The snowy peaks above Ladhak beckoned us to Thibet, and the forest about us wore russet and gold. Here autumn was very far advanced, yet people went about without feeling cold. Our ancestral home was a wooden structure reared on stone foundations. A family of Ladhaki farmers lived on the lower floor, with cows and goats in an outer shed. To our north, high hills rose like a menacing prison wall. In the east and the west we had some acres of land bounded by the steep and impeccable hills forbidding and fierce. Only to the south was there a view—fold upon fold of lower ridges thickly covered with timber till they dipped their feet in the lake. The stream that went by our little village of sixteen families was but a narrow arm of the lake that reached almost to our very door. Mornings and evenings were so cold that no matter where I went I carried under my tunic an earthen pot full of ashes in which burnt charcoal like embers in a brazier. That is all the heat people had all winter long except when they cooked, but that fire filled the house with smoke fit to blind the eyes. For not one house had a chimney.

Our first fortnight there it rained—not the hard thick shower of the south, but Chota barkha, a soft, sighing rain, soft as a panther's tread but persistent as a hungry mendicant. It pleaded day and night till at last we felt that it would drive us mad with its pleading. Our neighbours who visited us, shivering like wet hounds, suddenly began to speak in strange brief sentences. Fear was written on their white faces, and the more it rained the more they lowered their voices. In the north the people are very light. Their pale skin shocked me at first by its lack of colour. But I soon got used to it as I grew used to the milky twilights devoid of burning bright colours of the south.

That our neighbours were frightened beyond concealing it left no doubt in our mind. Now that the rain had gone on a fortnight they openly discussed flight, their white faces impressing me most terribly. They were not faces but masks of fear. A council of war was held in our house. Now I learned what the trouble was. The rain might bring a landslide.

In the Himalayas too much rain loosens mountains. Whenever that long sighing rain falls black and softly as a bat's wings, people take fear. It falls, but instead of rolling down the hills, it sinks to their roots and cuts them. With razor-sharp claws it burrows and burrows till root after root of a hill is cut. Then the rain pushes it an inch a day—Imagine a whole mountain moving thus. At last in a fortnight the precipice loses its balance and falls like a drunken titan, crushing under it men, women and children like so many pigmies and worms.

Though the whole village counseled flight, my aunt and I stayed on. One family after another left until we two were alone. At last one night the rain stopped, then began the first movement of a hill. We felt the house tremble. Then silence, deathwhite moonlit silence. Again the house trembled. Again the thrust of silence like a blade into our heart. Then instead of another quake of the house

—a terrific yell; all beasts, birds and thunders put together could not make such a noise. Our home throbbed very little. But we knew that our place had been saved. Kuri and I who were standing on the upper verandah clung to each other in terror and awe as we dragged ourselves within. Like the breathing of a babe, the earth sighed in relief, it seemed, and subsided.

Next morning we looked abroad; lo, a cavity of charred yellow mass had appeared in the east beyond our village; a small hill had been lifted and flung away as a child throws away an uprooted plant. And God in His infinite mercy had left our village untouched. In another day's time, our neighbours began to return one by one.

XIII—Tosa Shawls

AFTER the entire village had returned, life resumed its usual course for a few days. Then something most interesting took place. The harvests had already been brought in, and the thank-offering had been celebrated. Now the community turned its attention to another means of subsistence. In the old days before machine-run industries had put their tentacles into the vitals of our country, the peasants had two means of livelihood: agriculture and weaving. Each community had its own special art. Bengal wove muslins. Madras wove and printed calico. Rampur spun chuddars that were as flexible as water and as comfortable as our mother's hands. And Kashmere wove its shawls. Though other provinces are no longer producing their woven fabrics, Kashmere still frets the looms in order to embroider Dosalas (double shawls) and Zamewars (embroidered shawls).

The most precious shawls are made out of ibex wool. But there is one variety that is not made of any wool, yet people who wear it will say to you on their oath that the fabric on their back is made of no other substance. Such is the deception wrought by the skill of the Tosa shawl-makers.

What is Tosa made of? During the moulting season of the Tosa bird the village sends out a group of able-bodied young men to collect the feathers; out of them the shawl is made.

This particular year the birds had begun to moult in late September. The news was vouchsafed to us one day by the sight of a little white bird small as a swallow. He came and sat on our roof. I said to my aunt: "What a strange bird!"

She said: "Why, child, that is a Tosa." She looked at it very carefully.

"What is a Tosa, aunt?" I asked her.

"Its feathers when carded and cured are spun into thread for shawls. Look, he is not honey-coloured, but pure cream. He must have moulted recently."

While we were talking thus, the whole village had gathered near our home and were examining the "brother of the precious feather." When the bird flew away they said: "It is unusual for the Tosa to moult now, but sometimes it happens. Let us, therefore, go into the jungle and gather more feathers, which will add to the supply for the shawl-making this winter."

The same evening a council of the community was held in which the Tantiguru, or chief weaver, an old man of seventy and more, after listening to everybody, advised us on the morrow to start for the jungle. Since I insisted, I was allowed to join the band that consisted of nearly a dozen men. My aunt was glad to let me go.

Long before sunrise, after bathing in ice-cold water before eating any breakfast, we gathered at the village temple each with his week's supply of chhana (beans) on his back. There, after prayers and benediction from the lips of the priest, Tantiguru exhorted us:

"Beasts of prey will cross your path. But do not frighten them. Each day pray to God to keep you from fear. Do not frighten the birds either, for if you frighten the brother that yields the feathers, it will make him sick, and his feathers will not be as good. Only a healthy bird yields clean feathers. Fear makes disease. So go up to the nest when the brother is not there; gather all the feathers in your wallets, and leave the nest untainted with haste and pure of all human odours. Meditate 'May I be calm, may I be brave.' "

After that we said farewell to the ladies of the village and departed. All of us wore goat-skin coats to keep ourselves warm. The skins had fur on them more than an inch long. Our feet were sandalled in heavy leather cothurns.

Within a day's march we reached a small Balti settlement in the midst of the jungle. It consisted of two families of hard faced but kind hearted Baltis. They offered to put us up at a nominal charge per head. This Balti settlement we shall call Baltisthan (home of the Balti).

The following day with a handful of chhana in our pockets for lunch and our wallets slung from our shoulders, we entered the deeper jungle. How different it was from our southern woods! There were no tropical trees worth speaking of. Chestnuts thrust their roots like mammoth talons into the granite soil. Weeping ash trees let down their autumn gold boughs next to evergreens, stern as ascetics. Rowan trees and walnuts jostled each other in a harsh competition to reach the sun. Some plane trees battled steadily with linden for more air and space. Once in a while a gnarled oak contorted like a dancing deity.

It was on one of these oaks that we sighted a nest of Tosas. I went up and took from it a handful of its feathers. They were more silver than honey coloured. As I was leaving the nest I heard a bird scolding me from above. In the white sunlight he looked like the core of purity.

That day we all gathered feathers without trouble. But the test of our dexterity came the next day, for when we looked up into the nests that we had robbed of Tosa feathers the previous day, we found that many of the birds had not spent the night at home. That meant that we had frightened them away. Out of the half dozen nests that I had been robbing, only two yielded a few feathers; the others had nothing.

Now I am a man that loved not over much to meditate, but nevertheless I had now to spend the day in meditation. "May I never frighten the brothers. May their feathers be undiseased."

Whether it was this meditation or because the birds got used to us, they soon gave up keeping away from their nests, and in less than ten days' time each one of us had nearly a pound of feathers. As soon as our quota was completed, we returned home. I cannot begin to describe the joy of the women when they saw their men return unharmed by wild beasts.

The next day we repaired to the temple grounds and offered our quota to Tantiguru. Now I saw a thrilling sight. The ancient man took one sack of feathers at a time, and opening its mouth and thrusting his hands into it, he poured out handsful of feathers on the floor, diving like a hawk swooping and grabbing out any imperfect one that happened to be in that silver stream. What eyes and what agility!

After all the imperfect feathers had been winnowed out he handed over the good ones to the women of the village to spin and make threads.

Next week all the women spun. Sweetly their

bracelets tinkled and beat time to their singing while they tore and twisted the soft parts of each feather and spun them into threads. Singing like water ran through the village.

At last the day of weaving the shawl was decided upon, and all the weavers were asked to go without food if they could for the preceding twenty-four hours. I, too, wished to weave, so I decided to fast from sunrise to sunrise. During my fast Tantiguru came to see me. He looked taller than his usual six feet, for he had put on a long flowing toga whose lines heightened his stature considerably. His beard, like threads of white silk, and his bald head accentuated his age. He wanted to see me alone. So we went to the verandah where he put his two hands on my head and prayed:

"May your touch be so quickened that it will ache with Beauty. May your mind be free of greed and fear. May the warp and the woof be fixed in your soul so that your fingers will sing out the threads into pattern. Your hands—may they become eloquent as tongues!" After pausing a few moments he touched his own toga and illustrated. "Behold this garment! It was woven by my grandfather. Its colour is fast. The texture is as smooth as the skin of a child, yet how flexible. Examine its threads—yea, press them with your fingers, put your fist under it. Do you perceive the pattern?"

"Yes, my Lord."

"Good," exclaimed the ancient weaver. "Hold that design in your head till it sinks down into your mind and into your dream. As a man dreams so he weavcs. Farewell." He walked away not a poor village weaver but a poet-potentate—Kavyaraja.

On the following morning we performed our ablutions and prayed, and after a meagre breakfast of chapati (bread) and hot goat's milk, we assembled in Tantiguru's house.

In one of the well-lighted rooms the frame had been laid and the warp made ready and near it sat the master craftsman like a priest before his deity. Each one of us softly walked into the room and sat around the frame. Seeing that we were seated he called to the village virgins in the house to bring the threads they had spun. Unlike us, they walked ringing their anklets and talking to one another.

There were eight of them vestured in green, saffron, and violet silk saris, and they trooped in and out, leaving beside each weaver a spindle full of threads like gossamer.

"May you weave with song," commanded the master. "May your skill be such that the fabric that you make will be exquisite as moonlight, but as certain in effect as the thunderbolt."

Then the weaving began. I who knew very little of it had to watch them work. Thread after thread like the tongues of vipers flashed into sight and vanished. To watch their dexterity at weaving pained me, but the sense of pain in all craftsmanship is something that I consider a mark of its distinction. How those men's fingers pleaded with, pushed and pulled those gossamer strands will always remain to me inscrutable, yet simple. Sometimes they chided the thread with song:

"Come, come
Like a stream out of the rock;
Come, come
Like the serpent to the charmer's flute."

By the noonday siesta I had acquired enough art to pass on a thread that was handed to me. . . . I could quickly insert it in the warp and pull it through till it was ready for my neighbour's hand. How we ever kept the wholeness of the design in mind I cannot tell. Fifteen people were weaving one shawl. Of course all the others except myself were born weavers. Their fingers knew the design as a mother's hands know the weight of her child.

About three in the afternoon we began again. Song upon song was sung, sometimes in chorus, sometimes in a solo by a good voice while the rest worked in silence. The master weaver would touch someone with his hand or stick, to correct a false move. Towards the day's end he sang a long praise of shawls. He praised "The Jamewar (the embroidered shawl) for its dignity." The Alawan (the chuddar) he extolled "That ever present friend, sustainer of the body like our mother's milk." Then after hymning the multitudinous colours of a "Doshalu" (a double shawl), he ended with a short strophe on "Ashli" (the pure design) and the old time lac dye (red dye) washed in cream.

So on day after day. At last after six weeks the shawl was finished. With it a sadness fell upon us all. We who had wrought magic ceased to be sorcerers now. The last rite of the Tosa was sweet all the same. The shawl was folded and handed to the women of the village who measured it. "Six feet long and two and a half broad." At that announcement Tantiguru took off a ring from his little finger and passed the entire shawl through it. "It is well done, lo, it passes the test." A flash of joy suffused his face for a moment. "This ring was given to my ancestor by the emperor Shah Jehan, the builder of Taj Mahal. Ever since that time all our shawls must enter it with the humility of a slave and come out a master."

Now I touched the shawl; and I can swear that most people touching and feeling it will say what I said then: "It is not birds' feathers but made of wool. Is it not natural then that the weaving of such a fabric should exalt the maker to the rank of a wizard?" *

* To corroborate Ghond's story of Tosi or Kosi shawls made out of feathers, see the note on Tosi in "The Christian Science Monitor" of August 26, 1924, page 5. This paper is printed in Boston, Massachusetts, U. S. A.

XIV—The Tiger Tamer of the Circus

BEFORE snow had begun to fall, we left our home near Ladhack and began our journey towards Srinagar, which is a very beautiful city. The valley of Kashmir near Srinagar seems to be a chalice of beauty. Small wonder then that poets call the capital of Kashmir, Nagar, or town of Shri—beauty.

We reached there just after Dasahara or New Year. I must explain how we Hindus happen to have more than one New Year's day within six months of one another. All told, India observes four New Years. There is the Christian calendar that begins in the middle of the winter, then the Mohammedan almanac has its own way of marking the end of the year, and all Hindus keep up two eras, the Saka and Sambat; the former starts the year in the spring, and the latter in the autumn. We Hindus love festivals so much that we not only celebrate our two New Year's days, but we join the Christians and the Mohammedans in celebrating theirs.

It was, however, after our own Dasahara, autumn New Year, that we reached Srinagar in time to join in the Dipavali festival which comes ten days later.

All men know that half of the streets in the capital of Kashmir are but water-ways whose chariots are boats and barges. From the edge of Lake Dal into the very middle of the city the streams run in and out like silver paths losing themselves between wooden huts and stone mansions. It is very startling to arrive at a house by a boat and go out of it on an elephant from its other door.

Imagine to yourself the double splendour of the city during the evening of the Dipavali! All day the weavers had not woven shawls, the ivory carver had forsaken his workshop, even the hawkers were absent from streets and streams. Unlike most parts of Mohammedan-ridden India, here the Hindu women were free to go about, their faces uncovered in the company of their men folk. All day the city spent idling and amusing itself. Ere the sun went down, the royal procession of scores of elephants issued out of the palace gates. In the violet twilight through arches festooned with golden leaves they trod, solemnly raising their trunks in salutation to the balconies whence men and women in red, yellow, turquoise, saffron, white, purple, and amber saris greeted them. On both sides of the street were turbaned heads, Moslems in green and white, and Hindus in lavender, yellow, lilac, and ochre. Now the last elephant came into sight, carrying the Maharajah of Kashmir on its back: its tusks sheathed in gold, its head covered with pearls and its back and flanks wrapped in a cloth of gold from which the evening light streamed. A cavalcade of white horses and white clad riders followed the procession. As soon as they had passed, the crowd moved toward the water front ere it grew totally dark. There barges and boats decorated with artificial flowers and bunting were waiting. As their occupants took their seats, each barque slid out on the dark water, and lighted its lamps, and the boatmen began to sing.

Our own boatmen not only sang but they had tied strings of tiny bells around their four oars, so each one of their strokes poured music on the water. Thus we drifted under the starry sky hour after hour.

The following day in one of the open squares of the city we met the circus that we had seen weeks ago in Delhi. Curious to know what had happened to the tiger tamer we made enquiries. I must admit that I was more than surprised to find him performing in the afternoon.

After his performance was over we met and

asked him to have a ride with us in a boat. Thus began a momentous thing in my life, though at the time I did not foresee it. On the boat the tiger tamer told us his story. He had a long horse-like face whose expression never changed no matter what he spoke of. He had no beauty anywhere unless it dwelt in his eyes which also were like a horse's, benevolent and dull. Somehow he surmised at once that I was looking at him and appraising his character. And he said to my utter embarrassment, "My young examiner, do you not know that a man who deals with animals for years at last begins to look like one? I lived with horses, camels, leopards and tigers from babyhood. My father was a Santal chieftain whom the Rajah of the Central Province loved. Though we were pure of all the taints of civilisation, yet because the Rajah liked us, he used to leave many of his new horses in our jungle to train and rear. I believe I learned to crawl under the belly of Rita, the Arab mare, long before I crawled on the floor of our home. Do you see that mark on the nape of my neck? There Rita's baby colt stepped when I was eighteen months old. I was crawling under its mother when that fortnight-old fellow came to get some milk. Fortunately he only slashed my skin with his hoof, otherwise I should not be here to describe it.

"I think I sat on Rita the very first day my mother wanted me to sit up. I believe I was born on horseback. Even now I can sit on the wildest horse no matter in what position—facing either tail or head —without falling off.

"Then our family took to catching and training baby leopards for the Jadu Ghor, Zoological Gardens. I have known leopards as you know kittens. By the time I was twenty my father pushed me out of our house as a bird pushes off its fully fledged child. I took to the nearest town with my two bears that I had caught and trained. I showed them bear dances: '*Thoomook, Thoomook, Nachre Bhaluk*—Dance, dance O my bear.' Then I ran into a circus in a town where I was performing. Its owner employed me to play in his own company. So instead of leading bears all alone, I became part of a large show. One day, a year later, our tiger performer died. I had to perform with his animals and with mine in two separate acts. Later I sold my bears and performed only with the cats. I have been with those cats pretty nearly twenty years now. They are getting old and very fretful."

A few minutes after he had stopped speaking, I asked him: "How have you overcome your fear of those tigers since we saw you last?"

"What a leech-like memory you have, my son," he exclaimed sarcastically. "To tell you the truth I must thank you for advising me to cleanse myself of fear that day. After you had warned me I did what I should have done earlier. I gave up drinking and had my tiger's eyes washed."

"We do not follow," ejaculated my aunt.

"The reason my tigers hated me was that I had taken to drinking. The odour of grog irritated them, and I in turn began to be frightened. The more I was frightened, the more I drank. When you saw me first I was living on alcohol but as soon as you had warned me I stopped drinking. I gave out the story that I was sick. For a month I went away to my people in the woods with my animals. There we found that one of the tigers was going blind, his eyes hurt him terribly every time he faced the light. Poor fellow, he hated to perform night or day. We all searched, and at last found the eye herb whose juice washes away the films and the pain from the eyes of men or animals. In a fortnight he was out of pain and never snarled at anyone that came near him. My son, why don't you become a tamer of animals?" he asked me pointedly. The question surprised me. "You understand animals. Why not live for them and love them? Our dumb brothers are forced to live with too many fools and cruel people. Come, join the thinking ranks of the protectors of the beasts," he concluded.

Before we said farewell to him, he gave me his permanent address: "Some day you may like to come to me. Keep this address." With those words he got off our boat and vanished into the city of Srinagar.

The next day we left Kashmir for Rawal Pindi and home.

XV—The Were-Tiger

WE reached home about a week before Bara-din, or Christmas; Bara means big and Din day, or beginning of the longer days. On our way we stopped at Fatehpore, that city built by Akbar's order in the sixteenth century. I could not believe that because an emperor said "Build me a city," lo! there should arise like the goddess Shri (Beauty) from the ocean this paradise of marble, granite, and sandstone.*

From Fatehpore we went to Delhi, and then from Delhi to Jeypore. The last named city, too, was built at the command of a Hindu king, Jey Singh, who desired a town with straight streets and houses with one skyline. There it stands in Rajputana to-

* Shri is the Hindu equivalent of Aphrodite. The latter rose from the foam of the Mediterranean before a Phoenician barque that traded in gold and precious stones. Similarly Shri, the Goddess of beauty, wealth and virtue, rose out of the depths of the Indian Ocean and sat on the prow of a merchantman.

day. Elephants ply like hackney coaches between violet, purple, rose and white houses. Camels come and go, hundreds at a time like a tawny string drawn from the gold of dawn to the cobalt dusk of evening.

Every afternoon the young nobles take their walk between palaces like an ancient painting come to life. On housetops pigeons gleam in many colours as the sunset squanders its fabulous gold from the sky. In balconies red, white, yellow, and purple, women stand or sit dressed in sumptuous splendour, while below on the dun-coloured road walk groups of young men, some in purple togas, some in long flowing blue silk; next to them a small band in white, followed by a large crowd in orange, saffron, and green. Sometimes an elephant loaded with boys and girls walked silently along while its riders sang and chattered.

The enchanting short twilight is soon over, however, and the desert wind stirs up a blue haze that floats like incense smoke from street to street. Before it the pigeons fly from their housetops, the balconies empty and the streets are bereft of their procession. The only thing that keeps a touch of magic about it is the colour of the palaces, the pleasure gardens and the fountains over which the blue night hovers like a bird. If you ever go to Jeypore, do not forget to look at it for as many hours of sunset as you can.

After a week there we started homewards, and though we had seen many beautiful things during these months, both my aunt and I were glad to behold the smoke from the Mayavati houses rise against the sky at whose northern edge sat the Himalayas like priests at their evening worship. As we drew nearer we heard women singing at their work and men putting the finishing touch to their day's toil. Just then, I know not how, a sense of melancholy seized my entire being.

That one should experience the sadness of evening is natural, but I had never felt it before. It took me fifteen years on earth before I fell a happy prey to the lifting and healing melancholy of the evening hour.

That night Purohit came to welcome us back to Mayavati. According to our Indian custom we had brought a present for everybody in the village. We gave the priest the illuminated manuscripts of the Gita, Song of God, our Bible, which we had purchased at Jeypore. It was so beautiful that the priest could not speak as he turned the thick parchment pages of the book and scanned the illumination on each page. This was one of the old, old arts in India which foreigners learned from us and carried abroad centuries ago. I shall never forget the illustration with which each half of a page was wrought, massive with colours as if it was cut out of red, yellow and blue rocks, yet the delicate lines with which it was drawn were thin as gossamer and hard as steel. "What art!" After saying that aloud, the priest added, "You have acquired merit."

After he had left I wondered why in India the

bestower of a gift has to content himself with the thought "Now that I have given I have acquired merit." Rarely one hears any kind of "Thank you" from the receiver. It was later, when I was past thirty, that an Englishman thanked me for saving his life from an elephant in the jungle. I said to him in answer: "I have acquired merit." At that he looked at me as if I were speaking in an unknown tongue.

Our first morning in Mayavati we spent in carrying our presents to different houses. My aunt said: "You see, the more you give away what you have, the more you lose selfishness. He who loses self becomes nearer God, and he who is nearer the Infinite through acquiring merit will, when he dies, be reborn in a better world. Never cease to acquire merit."

But I did not inform Kuri that the more merit I acquired by carrying presents from house to house, the more blisters I got on my feet.

Though the process of losing selfishness was making my feet ache, yet I did carry Prasad, spiritual present, to Kalu the grocer whom I never liked. In his house for the first time in my life I heard of the *Were-Tiger*. His shop was the echo board of all the gossip of our community; in fact the grocer had a superb sense of acoustics. No matter what was said in the secret places of Mayavati, one heard in a short time an amplified echo of it from Kalu's lips.

It was while he received the Prasad that he told me of the Man-Tiger. He pursed his thick lips and began:

"You have brought me Prasad.* And by it you have acquired endless merit! Prasad or food of Spiritual Communion, is a better present than other things. Ha! You received it at the temple of Brahma (the Creator) at Ajmeer? The priest blessed this rice and consecrated it? Good. It is therefore real Prasad. My whole household will eat it in order to purge our souls of many sins." He paused a moment as he laid the Prasad aside. "By the way, have you heard that Chamar, the cobbler of our village, has become a were-tiger?" Then he looked at me silently.

"What is a were-tiger, Mr. Kalu?" I asked him.

"Don't you know, O jungle-man of our village? I see that our priest has not taught you everything. Your ignorance does you credit. It has made you humble. Don't be impatient. A were-tiger is a man who goes out at night, walks on all fours, kills animals, and eats them raw. Chamar has been seen to do this for the past two full-moons."

"Who saw him?" I questioned. "Why did he go out in the light of a full moon?"

"Ha, you are a sceptic. The sorcery that turns a man into a tiger cannot be practised except on the occasion of a fully lighted night. I assure you that he turns himself into a tiger in order to kill cattle from whom he takes the hide next day. I believe he is a were-tiger. That is why I give him the widest berth if I see him after sundown."

* Prasad, like holy bread, is blessed by the priest in the temple. A piece of it may then be taken to anyone toward whom it is desired to express good will.

Though I did not believe most of what the grocer told me, yet his tale gave appetite to my curiosity. That day I went out and told the priest all about it. He did not place any faith in such a tale, surmising that some mean and malicious soul had started the damaging rumour against our good cobbler simply because two oxen had been killed by a tiger on a night of the full moon.

"But," I said, "the proverb enjoins: 'An elephant-large rumour is founded at least on a mouse-small fact.' "

"Well, what do you wish to do about it?" asked Purohit. "Do you wish to disembowel the elephant in order to discover the little fact?"

"But are were-tigers true, my Lord?"

"No," he answered with the utmost conviction. "Rumour of tiger-men I have heard, but never could I find that it was true. There is no such thing, save in the malicious minds of mean folk."

"My Lord, let us investigate it!" I begged him.

"So that is it, you seek amusement? Well, let us avoid boredom by pursuing this matter, it may be entertaining. The night of the next full moon we will go after Chamar! Will that satisfy your appetite for adventure?"

After I had bade the priest good-bye, I went to Chamar's house. There was nothing unusual there! He was working hard at his trade. He was the cobbler, shoe-maker and tanner for the entire community. In the front yard of his hut lay all kinds of skins drying in the sun. Within, in a small room he was drying a piece of leather for the purpose of making vermilion slippers. He hummed a tune while he did his work. I sat near him on the floor and talked. The odour of leather is never pleasant; all the same I stayed as long as was necessary for a general description of my recent tour. He looked at me now and then as he listened and toiled; his large mouth, fox-like eyes, small chin and spacious brow, as I examined them casually, betokened nothing sinister. This fellow did not remotely resemble a tiger-man, besides, he had the reputation of being a good husband and a very kind father. In spite of that the priest and I lay watching for him on the night of the next full moon. and we did not have long to wait either.

About ten o'clock when the whole village had gone to sleep, Chamar emerged from his house. He looked all around very carefully. Then he listened to the sounds of the night which were many. Despite the terrible cold of the winter, many insects were talking to the moon. Far off the phao—a species of fox—cried, which meant, as it always does, that the tiger was near by.

But nothing daunted Chamar. He set out in the direction of the jungle, and, of course, we followed but at a considerable distance, owing to which we lost sight of him within half an hour near a bush.

Then we heard "phao, phao, phao," almost at our feet. We went towards the sound, but since we could see nothing owing to the thick vegetation, we climbed a tree in order to see clearly. Lo, down there, hardly a dozen yards from where we stood, a jackal was phaoing and shivering in an ecstasy of terror. In the moonlight he looked like the white ghost of a dog howling which convinced us that a *sher* (meaning tiger), was near. It is a common fact of the jungle that whenever these jackals smell tiger, they are hypnotised by the fear of *sher,* and howl like demons. This annoys the big cats, and since they don't eat phao they either go away from the neighbourhood of the yelling lunatic, or, come near him and roar; which at once silences the wretched animal and makes him run as fast as his legs can carry him.

The latter is exactly what happened now. In a few minutes the saplings and bush behind the howler parted. The moonlight vibrated through the shaken heavy dew. Like the radiant face of a demoniac deity, the white head of a tiger came into view. "Gr-r-r—rhaool," he roared. If there is any sound that pierces the ears and instantly penetrates to the inmost soul it is the full-throated cry of a tiger. There is no sound as compelling in nature, not even the trumpeting of a mad elephant.

That instant, as if a spell has been broken, the phao stopped shivering, and his heart-rending shriek was stilled. "Whao" barked the tiger at him once more. The wretched fox fled so quickly and so softly that not even a plant moved to indicate the direction he had taken.

The tiger moved forward. More than half of him stood exposed to our view. He appeared wrapped in a halo of flashing pearls. The moonlight striking the shaken and falling dew wrought an indescribable witchery around him. Now he raised his head and looked up at our tree. His eyes seemed to fasten on ours. He gazed and gazed; and as he did so he changed. Inch by inch his jaws and nose altered. Then suddenly these emerald eyes became red like those of a very angry man's. Slowly his receding brow thrust itself forward. . . . It was ghastly, that head of a man in the body of a brute. Suddenly he opened his mouth and yelled. In that terrible growl of a beast of prey, we heard the cry of a man. It was the most sinister sound imaginable. It smote me like a javelin of terror. My knees shook under me, and my teeth chattered in my head. The priest, in order to save me from falling down, put his hand around my waist and whispered in a calm tone of assurance: "It is only a frightened tiger." I was gripped by a feeling of nausea. I shut my eyes and with the shutting of my eyes I made a tremendous effort to control my legs and knees which had begun to give way utterly. In a moment, feeling more steady, I opened my eyes. Lo, there was nothing on the ground! The moonlight was falling like a cascade, and all nature was heavy with sleep. No animal of any sort could we see or hear. Had I really dreamed, standing there on the tree, or was I awake? We heard a far-off roar in the direction of the village, and that was all. Nothing more eventful happened that night. As soon as day broke like a crust of ice, an opaque light came through a cloud in the east. We descended from our perch. Very few birds sang. An owl hooted, a marten yawled, and a wild rooster struck out a staccato rejoinder which was drowned by some freezing peacock shrieking at the sun for more warmth. But of warmth there was none. When we got to the ground we were drenched with dew heavy as large melting hail. It was so moist and cold that whatever we touched rained down showers. Everything was humid and disagreeable. Slowly we crept to the bare spot where the Phao had sat and shouted. Yes, in spite of moisture, there lay on the grass a clear mark of his haunches, and there where the tiger-man had emerged lay the pugs of a large cat. We had not been dreaming of the beast. But the terrible thought of the man came to my mind. Was it our cobbler? Or— "A beast is a beast, brother," I heard the priest counseling. "Do not be deluded. It can be nothing else. The unearthly moonlight touches a man's imagination and he thinks that he has seen a tiger-man, and that is why we think we see him only during the intensely bright nights."

"I can wager, my Lord," I challenged, "he will issue forth tonight, too, as he did last night."

"We shall see," concluded the priest.

Now we followed the tiger's trail all the way to the village, and by our house to our own cowshed. Lo, the door of it had been flung open, and only a hundred yards away from it lay a slain cow! By its face, which was not mutilated, I identified my pet Goma.

The rest of our cattle had run away none knew whither. The stampede must have been terrific when the tiger's paw smote the door of the cow-shed and flung it open after the bolt had broken under the stroke. No tiger had ever broken the lock of a cowshed before, in order to plunder its valuable beasts. The act of breaking open the heavy door made it seem like the work of a man.

A keen sense of pain pierced me as I examined the scene, particularly when I stared at poor slain Goma's lustreless eyes. She had been my friend from childhood—in fact my very dear pet. There she lay dead and mutilated.

"Look, what is this?" exclaimed the priest. "How strange; the footprints of a man!"

Indeed there were the marks of a man's bare feet leading away from where the cow was killed towards the jungle. But stranger still, almost parallel to him lay the pugs of a tiger whose blood-stained claws had left marks on the ground for at least a score of yards.

"Extraordinary!" Purohit thought aloud; "tigers are clean animals, they lick themselves free of the least taint of their hunt before they go home after their feed. How can it be that this animal, like a careless human butcher, leaves blood-marks on its trail? This needs studying. Let us get out into the woods before the whole village wakes. We must not let anyone learn of our activity. This way—come quickly. Do you hear the village? They have found out that the tiger has been visiting our hamlet."

We reached the temple running by a circuitous path, a few minutes before the village elders and my aunt had started thither looking for the priest. They were glad to learn from the latter that I had been with him and not lost.

They held a joint conference on the nature of our

cow's death. Everyone had seen marks of human feet, along with the tiger's pugs. The priest did not divulge to them the secret of the two human feet that had left their prints on the wet grass. He urged the village not to appear more than normally agitated and to make no capital out of the were-tiger legend. He enjoined them to be calm. "If we wish to pierce the secret of all this murderous business, we must keep silent and work in secret. I swear to you that in a few days the reality of this situation will float like a corpse on the waters of our investigation."

You may ask what our servants and workers were doing? They had gone after the stampeding herd, which was the reason why no one was at home when the priest and I reached the scene early in the morning. It took the poor fellows the whole forenoon to round up all the animals. When they came back, men and beasts were utterly spent.

Now, as is the custom of Hindu villages, we went to the cobbler's and asked him to come to our place in order to dispose of the carcass. He was still sleeping, which roused our suspicion; we felt that only a man who had been out all night would sleep so late. It was one more proof that he was a were-tiger. He sent word from his bedroom that he would come as soon as he had finished his toilet.

When he did appear at our place I was fast asleep in my bed after the night's strenuous work. The priest had told me to sleep well, for the coming night might be so well lighted by the moon that it would tempt the tiger to sally forth.

According to Purohit's instructions after the sunset, I went to a particular spot in order to keep watch on the cobbler's house. Toward half past nine, Purohit joined me in spite of a touch of rheumatism that he had caught the night before. We watched and waited for Chamar to go on his night's hunt. The light was so bright that one could hardly tell that the moon was not full.

Behold, about ten o'clock Chamar again set out on his night's chase. This time we kept him in sight. No matter how deep he went into the jungle, we pursued him unfalteringly, apparently he suspected nothing, for he never looked back. He seemed quite sure that he was alone. Presently from the heart of the jungle he turned back, going around about in the direction of our village. Reaching a certain spot he got up a tree and stayed there. We followed his example and made ourselves secure on another tree. Hardly half an hour had passed when came the usual tiger sounds; snap, crack, crack; no doubt a big cat was stepping on dry leaves. In a few moments more there stood a tiger under Chamar's tree. It circled about then for the village; we could tell by its roar the direction in which the monster had gone. We followed the tiger believing that he was a man-tiger. I believed that through an art of fine sorcery the man had turned himself into a beast. That is why we never dreamed of watching Chamar's tree after the tiger had set out for the village. Even the old priest half-believed the transformation by now.

We got down from our perch and went to the

temple to spend the night there. Next morning as we had anticipated, another cow, this time it was Kalu's the grocer's; his only cow had been killed exactly in the same fashion as our Goma. What was most startling was that human foot-marks were discernible on the track that bore the tiger's.

Kalu, a money-loving tradesman, lost his temper and almost lost his mind over his cow's death; so he hastened to Chamar's house and openly accused him of being the killer. "You are," he shouted, "a tiger-man! You murder the cows at night in order to profit by flaying and grabbing their skins by day. You make money at the cost of the community! You pay us not a penny! On the contrary we pay you for removing the rotting carcass from our door, and you make double profit! You are a tiger-man at night and a cobbler by day! A curse on your head! May the gods scald your gizzard with molten lead!"

The cobbler howled with rage. He called the grocer a liar and a cut-throat of a money-lender. "May the gods," he wailed, "cut your stomach open and fill your insides with perpetual fire. You lie. I am not a *sher*. I am a man."

But the upshot of the quarrel was that nobody went near the cobbler. The whole village boycotted him. It was owing to this open quarrel between himself and the grocer that now Chamar never went out at night. The entire community kept such a strict watch on him that he was never again seen to go near the forest. This was a great pity, for it prevented our discovering the exact nature of the were-tiger legend. Supposing that by some magic he really could take on the nature of a *sher,* it was unwise to offend him. It would have been far better to learn from him, no matter at what expense, the secret of his power.

Before the next full moon had come, the boycott had made his life so unbearable in our village that Chamar and his entire family left it for some other place. No one knows whither he went and what trade he took up. But did the tiger stop coming, after Kalu had openly accused the cobbler of being a were-tiger? No. Two more cows were killed in the same fashion as before, with this important difference however: there were no human footprints on the animals tracks. Then, suddenly, it all stopped. Even to this day no one can explain that were-tiger affair to my satisfaction. This was the only incident of its kind that I ever came across in my entire life. Since that time I have always hoped to find another place where such a thing had happened in order to track the mystery to its real source. Alas! God has never granted me my wish.

XVI—Some Pet Animals

I HAVE already mentioned that our priest taught me during my childhood a great deal about animals. But he never encouraged me to tame them. With the exception of a dog I never knew any domesticated animals save cows, camels, and elephants. Our house did not even have a half-wild cat in those days.

But after I had seen Santal of the circus play

with three tigers, I decided to have animals of my own in order to do tricks with them. Before one can do tricks one must own some beasts, and since trapping them was distasteful to me, I had to find an animal in some other way.

Fortunately I had not very long to wait. About the middle of February I acquired a mongoose, whom I found wandering helplessly in the woods. He was about a week old. It was not the season for mongoose to have babies, so instead of letting him go its way to certain death by starvation I brought him home with me, assuming that its parents were dead.

I fed him on milk, cheese and other vegetarian diet for the first fortnight or so, then I let him wander and catch baby snakes during the early summer when the spring eggs had been hatched.

It was from one of his expeditions after snakes that he returned to us with another mongoose. The latter was stronger, older, and extremely chary of human company. I inferred that the big one was a friend of our Benji, the little mongoose. The older animal rarely came to the house. She would approach as far as the courtyard, play with the little fellow awhile, then bid him farewell, as his bedtime drew near. Occasionally at sunset, both of them went up a large haystack in the open and sat there most silently meditating upon the day's end. In fact Mongoose senior seemed to instruct Benji in the art of sitting still until the dusk had taken possession of the far spaces. There was nothing surprising in all this in India, where men and women pray, meditate, or hold some religious rites during sunrise and sunset. I firmly believe that as the human beings act so do some of the animals of a country. Religion is not man-made. Animals, too, achieve it.

One day about the middle of June, when it was very dry, Benji went off early in the morning. He did not put in his appearance again for nearly six months. We all came to the conclusion that we had lost him. He had gone back to the wild. I who had given him freedom did not mind his return to nature, though it was very difficult to find another like him. By now I had a dozen homing pigeons, a pair of rabbits and a panther cub to look after, which filled my days. I had a dog also, but I never counted him as a charge. His name was Sarameya; for brevity's sake we called him Sar.

One may not feel the loss of a mongoose, but it is very hard to fill his place. No other animal is like him. Sar, the wolf-dog, missed him very much. Sar shared his grandfather's savage wolf-trait and used to run away into the forest with Benji. Now that the latter had gone the dog was very unhappy. Half the time he did not know what to do with himself. He hung around the village as most dogs do, and ran toward the jungle once in a while to find out if Benji was returning home. It was a pitiful dog that we had to deal with for nearly a month, who was either running up the stairs or going out of doors in order to look all over the countryside for the signs of the returning mongoose. Next to Sar, the pigeons felt the absence of the lost one most keenly. He was their playmate. Even the dog could not play his game of hide and seek so well. It would begin with a cheeping sound away below stairs. That meant: "Pigeons, are you ready?" These birds would look at one another, preen their wings and say nothing. "Cheep" from below again. The pigeons looked more unconcerned than ever, yet they kept their eye on the stairway. But did the mongoose come? Not yet. He was no such fool. The pigeons felt that the sound had no meaning for them. "It was a mistake; Benji was talking to someone else probably," each bird said to himself. Instead of expecting the mongoose, they set to amuse one another. Hardly had the pigeons relaxed their vigilance when like a black lightning up the stairs the little fellow dashed, his nose all point and his eyes red as burning charcoal. The pigeons hopped up and fled the roof as if from a hawk. The game had begun. No matter where and when a pigeon descended from the air, Benji would chase him off ere his two feet touched the roof. Then a very daring pigeon would swoop down; at that Benji would leap up to catch him, but alas, the four-footed fellow always fell short of his objective. He never caught even a feather.

Now there was no one to play with. The dog did his best to chase the pigeons off the roof, but his body was so big that he never could run fast on it. He seemed to reach the end of the roof before he got into any proper speed. Besides, these pigeons were forever running away. They did nothing for him. Truth to tell, they were a bit afraid of Sar. His height and length and his long jaws made him appear formidable, while Benji was small, and looked innocent. But the pigeons did not know that the sharp teeth of the mongoose could do more damage than those of a dog. Besides, Sar was trained not to hurt any domestic animal, be it a cat, a bird, or an albino rat.

Sar, however, did have one real playmate in another animal. I have already mentioned a baby panther. She was bought for me by my aunt as a present. We got her from a Yarkandhi trader who came by our village. She, the little kitten, we named Mita, the friend, and we taught her to love our big dog.

When Benji went away to the jungle, Mita was seven weeks old. Her coat was taking on that spotted magnificence that surpasses description. The gleaming gold skin was dotted with delicate and numerous deep brown spots; though they were small yet their abundance made them gleam like round black butterflies on yellow silk. And when she, the wearer of such a coat, went up a tree, the foliage hid her completely: she melted into its brown, green and yellow as if she was a part of the branch on which she crouched.

Even the keen eyes of the dog Sar could not make out where she hid. So he would howl and call for some sign of her. And, invariably, after a long spell of pleading from the foot of the tree, he got from above an awe inspiring "yawl"—a mixture of mewing and roar. Though inexplicable, yet that answer had something peremptory about it. It sent the dog away from under the tree. Was it that the cat made the dog understand by her cry that at heart her race was not a friend of his? Or was it purely the female cutting short the male's serenading. All the same, there was no hiding that something doleful dwelt in that cat's spirit.

What did I do about training her? First of all, she never had any uncooked food to eat, and instead of meat of any sort, she was given cooked fish. Even mutton and chicken were unknown to Mita until she was six months old.

Two things are taught to an animal, namely the taste for blood, and fear. Very few creatures are born with a love of either. Our purpose in training Mita was to keep her away from fresh meat, and since our little community in Mayavati had sheep, cows, chickens and pigs it would have been disastrous for the panther cub to acquire a taste for their flesh, raw or cooked, but since a cat must have some kind of carcass for its dinner we chose to give her fish, and even that was never uncooked. I can swear to it that had it not been for founding Mita's taste on such a diet, she would very early have killed chickens or sheep for the relish of their blood. Had she done so she could not have gone about freely in Mayavati.

XVII—Fatal Lesson of Fear

NOW that I have told you about the inception of my acquiring animals for pets, I will unfold to you the most dramatic experience that I had with my cat. It was in fact a fatal incident.

Mita, when about half a year old, took to staying on trees habitually. With the exception of her hours of meals and play with Sar, the dog, she was rarely seen on the ground. On the tree she kept up a life of her own. Sometimes I would go up one of the huge mango trees near our house to find out whether she was sharpening her claws, or just sitting still. For a long stretch of time she would lie on a bough and look down at the ground watching most intently for something. I have no doubt that she herself did not quite know what she was seeking. Her feline instinct was making her act a part as if in a play. Instinct it was that held her on the branch and made her think that she was watching for a prey. So every time Sar passed under the tree she would raise her shoulders and bend her legs in the perfect gesture preparatory for leaping on her victim. And after he had gone away, inch by inch, spot by spot, she would relax and go back to her original position, to that unconcerned concern of looking and watching the ground.

One evening while she lay on the mango tree, I too decided to sit on a neighbouring branch. The air was dry, the sky clear and cobalt blue. Our cattle were coming home raising dust like a golden incense smoke against the not distant forest. As she saw them draw nearer, the panther's eye changed colour. There was no more that agate-amber serene gaze. A flash of red had tinged the light in her eyes, her pupils glinting with a harsh look of concentration.

As the cows drew under our tree the colour of their hot bodies rose like fume to Mita's nostrils. Now I noticed that her eyes were all red and ere one could do anything to stop her, she howled like a maniac. This frightened the cattle; some of them jumped away from under the tree, lashing the cat's desire to attack. Like the coiling of a purple-black wire, her body rose and shrank into the size of a large ball. The leaves of the tree shivered—nothing more than that; they did not shake nor give out any sound until she sprang. But I had no eyes for the tree now. By accident she had fallen on the neck of an ox who was the last member of the herd. The surprise made him stop still for a moment, but as Mita's claws pierced through the skin and the yoke-made callouses of his neck, the pain acted like an electric shock. The bull's tail stood erect in the air like a ramrod. His head went down and down till it nearly disappeared between his forelegs. Mita was on the point of sliding down his bending neck, so she dug her claws and teeth deeply and securely into him. With an angry bellow of pain, he flung up his head and dashed forward. The force was so great that the small body of the six-months' old cat rose in the air like a ball and fell about four yards away. If only then the bull had stood facing the cat! Instead, he turned away and ran home like a coward. The cat raced after him toward the door of our compound, but seeing that it was impossible for her to overtake him she leaped and ran up a tree, and when I came under it and called her, the only answer I got was an angry growl.

It left no doubt in anyone's mind that Mita had learned the first lesson in fear: namely, that though small she could frighten an animal much bigger than herself. Her second lesson in fear came soon enough. It was taught her by the same bull.

One morning four or five days later our dog and

the cat were playing hide-and-seek in the field outside the house when the cows were being driven forward by the herdsmen. They were going in an utterly slack formation, so in order to play with them, the dog barked after the cattle. Following his example the cat too started to tease them. But the ox to whom she had taught fear, dashed out of the flock and chased her. She was so close that he could have trampled on her, but her feline resourcefulness saved her life. She leaped away. He, instead of following his original direction, swerved round, a most unusual thing for any cow to do, and attacked anew. Mita, panic-stricken, ran for her life. Of course, the bull desisted after a while; he forgot all about her in ten minutes and rejoined his herd, but the damage that he had done was irreparable. He had succeeded in completing Mita's lesson of fear. It had entered her soul. No one could find her during the next twenty-four hours. Whenever an animal is frightened, particularly a cat, it runs away to get over its disgrace. In the case of a feline such an experience of disgrace remains forever in its character and memory. Fear may take some time to teach, but once it has been learned it can rarely be shaken out of a creature. In the case of a man, thought can be re-educated and through thought his own character can be recast. But animals who are mostly victims of their own habits, unless we, their man-friends, take infinite pains, are rarely de-habituated. More than man, an animal's character is but the sum total of its habits. These are formed by violent emotions such as fear.

In another week's time, Mita had taken up her residence in trees. She always came down during the dusk in order to eat a solitary meal of boiled fish. No one saw her on the ground except after sundown and it became increasingly difficult to chain her up for the night. She scratched me twice as I tried to slip on her muzzle.

Now that the mangoes had ripened, monkeys came from all directions to the mangoes of our village. They came at first to our trees, not knowing who dwelt there. At last one night we heard the terrific howl of a panther and the shriek of consternation of the monkeys. Since nothing could be done in the dark, we waited till dawn.

In the morning light we found out that Mita had slipped off her muzzle and run away. The rest you can surmise. She had killed a monkey and eaten parts of it. Though it is horrible, I must explain certain details. In spite of the fact that she had never eaten anything but cooked food, and though she had never hunted and been taught to eat the most succulent portions of her victim's body, yet when I examined the remains of the wretched monkey, I found that she had eaten its throat, shoulders, chest and parts of the belly. It was a big male baboon that she had killed. How cowardly she was! It was her fear that told her to attack at night when the powerful eyes of a cat see almost as clearly as an owl's, while a monkey is nearly stone blind; otherwise she would not have dared to tackle a baboon nearly double her size.

But I could not speculate any further that morning, for vultures, those scavengers of God, were thundering down the air to remove the carcass in their own fashion. Without waiting for our new village cobbler who had just come to live in Chamar's place, one of our hired men and I carried the mutilated corpse to the Gobhagar or the field of offal nearly half a mile away from the village. It is needless to explain that every village has its Gobhagar or dead cattle's field where human beings go to leave to the vultures the remains of their dead friends, the beasts.

Ever since Mita's killing of that wretched baboon most of the monkeys fled our village for the season. Human beings breathed easily, therefore, as now they would not have to chase the tree-dwellers from their mangoes. That year we had a very large crop of mangoes. I suppose we should have thanked my panther for saving our fruit from the baboons.

She was not to be seen anywhere for three days after her monkey-feast. She had eaten too much to be hungry, for boiled fish, but on the latter part of the third day she put in an appearance a little before twilight. Sar, the dog, went to meet her as he saw her coming toward the house. The cat seemed to be in a benevolent mood. She played hide-and-seek for nearly fifteen minutes with a gusto that reminded us of her kitten days.

Then she came to her supper. While she busied herself with her fish, the wretched dog instead of letting her alone started to play at robbing her of her food. My aunt and I who were standing nearby scolded him and sent him away. But he returned to play with her, and instead of barking and annoying her gently, he dashed at her as if to challenge and rob her of her supper. With a sinister snarl Mita shot out her paw and slashed his neck; blood spurted out. That acted like a goad on both of them. Sar buried his teeth into her other paw while she bit into his shoulder and with another stroke of her paw ripped off his skin.

My aunt held her by her hindquarters and tried to pull while I hit her with her chain and muzzle. I hit, and hit and hit. Then flinging the dog away from her, she scratched my aunt's arm and fled into the night.

Let us spare ourselves many unpleasant details. That cat had almost done her worst before she gave up Sar. She had slashed his neck and shoulder with her paw. It seemed like a miracle that his throat was not slashed open. He would have bled to death had not our village veterinary come with the priest as soon as he was sent for, and he saved the poor dog's life. The doctor attended to my aunt's wound. Her arm was bleeding profusely. He dressed it very carefully, and before he left he said: "It is fortunate, Madam, that you escaped with a slight scratch."

The next morning the priest and some other villagers went forth to lasso the panther in order to put her in a cage.

News was brought to me at home that she had attacked one of the herds of sheep of the new cobbler and killed it, and she was nowhere to be found.

My aunt in the meantime grew worse and worse.

Hour by hour it became evident that her illness was not at all negligible. In a couple of days her pain became unbearable. How such a small wound could cause such an enormous swelling of her arm our village doctor could not make out. The more pain she suffered the more frightened he became. He advised the priest and myself to take her to a specialist. We placed her aching feverish body on a litter and had her carried to the nearest railway station, and thence by train to the city of Lucknow. There we found a blood specialist who, alas, pronounced the death sentence on her. Though the wound was negligible, it was fatal. He told the priest and myself: "It is not the wound but the germ that the panther's paw inserted in it that has done the mischief. Generally tigers, leopards and panthers lick themselves clean after their meals, but very often decaying meat of their prey sticks between their claws; there it rots and becomes a nest of deadly germs. Sometimes a scratch of a cat's paw no matter how superficial, lodges the germs of death from between its claws into the body of the person attacked. That is exactly what your panther has done to your aunt."

As soon as it became clear that she was not going to live, we tried to do whatever she wished. The only favour she asked was that we should take her to the holiest city of India, Benares, where she hoped to breathe her last, for it is said that those who die in a sacred city die with very noble thoughts in their mind.

The doctor said: "It is a long journey. You cannot go there."

"I promise not to die until I reach there," she answered.

By her voice I knew that her will was stronger than death. I had known that touch of firmness in her tone. If her voice ever took on that colour of determination she could and would do whatever she had set her mind upon. The priest knew that to be true. A descendant of the ancient warriors, she never failed to carry out whatever she promised. So we decided to start for Benares on the morrow.

It was there that the priest and I heard that Mita, my pet panther, had been trapped by our own herdsmen. And the village council of elders decided to sell the animal to the owner of a circus.

But the news of the cat's fate sounded like the echo of a lost sound to me. I was too busy nursing my dear aunt from whose body life was ebbing out drop by drop.

XVIII—GUNGA YATRA (DEATH BY THE GANGES)

WE reached Benares in twenty hours, about the middle of the night. Our patient was sinking so fast that we took her straight to the bank of the Ganges where she wished to breathe her last. After leaving me in charge of her the priest went in search of a doctor.

It was a cloudy night slowly clearing and revealing larger and larger starry patches over the river that murmured and moaned at the foot of the ghaut. There I waited for the coming of the doctor. Now and then Kuri groaned, half in delirium and half in pain.

All the multitudinous ghauts were deserted. Save for the hungry wail of a dog, nothing broke the devouring loneliness that was hemming us in. I listened for footsteps, alas, in vain. Kuri regained consciousness for a moment and asked for a drink. I ran down to the river, scooped up a little water and ran up again to her. After she had swallowed the last drop something moved, like a light; standing between her and me. It seemed to say to me: "Grieve not." That instant she passed out of her body, and then an extraordinary thing happened. Can I make it clear to you? Instead of the stunning silence of death I felt as if my aunt had become most eloquent. She was telling me ten thousand things at once. She was nearer to me now than she had ever been before. She and I were intimate beyond description.

Just when my Oneness with her was most complete, I heard someone walking around the dead. Slowly the departing spirit let go, and lo, I was pushed back into this world. A ghastly sensation of desolation seized my heart. Now I heard distinctly a stranger, the doctor, saying to the priest that it was all over. I do not know how much time elapsed; the next thing I remember is the carters bringing in loads of wood in their cart and the priest chanting. Apparently the doctor had seen to every arrangement, but I had no eyes for the logs; only my ears were alert. I heard the priest repeating:

"Birthless, deathless, changeless is the soul.
He who thinks It dies knows not the truth.
How can It die when It never condescended to be born?
It is above change, It is above death, It is coeval
with God."

With the help of the carters we piled the logs up, and made them into a high bed, and slowly and carefully placed the dead upon it. We covered her with piles of sandalwood topped with ordinary timber. Though my heart was breaking, since I was her nearest relative I had to perform the last rites. I lit a brand and walked around the fire seven times, praying as the priest directed me:

Akasastu niralamva
Vayu bhoota nirasraya

Now you are homeless in the heavens:
The wind, the earth, and all the living worlds
Can hold you no more.

* * * * *

Go, go to the realm of Eternal Life
whence you came!
The fathers of the race,
The Divine Elders, greet you.
Put on the vesture of God's effulgence
On star-strewn vales between rivers of light go
And dwell forever there where
all longings are fulfilled.

Now I applied the brand to the pyre and lighted it. The flames rose high as the smoke was blown away by the wind.

Not far off from where we were cremating the dead, the pilgrims, thousands at a time, came down long steps of the ghauts to take their morning dip before going to the temples to worship God at sunrise. Everything seemed sombre to me. It was not a city but a beehive of melancholy that hemmed around me.

At last, at about midday, there where had been

fire now lay a handful of ashes. These I gathered and flung on the stream of the Ganges:

> "Go, go on currents of rushing purity to the House of God where all is Peace and Perpetual Life."

At that moment I felt as if something had broken within me. A slowly descending arc of blackness covered and obliterated the fields across the river, the river itself, and last of all the very steps of the ghauts on which millions of people were standing. Darkness pressed on darkness until I saw nothing, smelt nothing, and felt—yes, I did feel as if a fly were crawling on my bare legs, and wherever it moved a perfect stillness followed. At last nothing but stillness rose like waters above my head. Far off something buzzed for a moment. Then that too was stilled.

According to the priest I was stricken with plague. I lay between life and death for hours. All I remember is that whenever I regained consciousness I felt as if my aunt sat there brooding over me, and with her I beheld the bent face of the priest. He tried everything to save me. First he tried an English doctor and his pure European medical science. It proved of no avail. Next he tried a Hakim. Hakimi is the medical science of the Indian Moslems. In spite of its great repute, it could not save me. Then Purohit tried our own ancient Hindu medicine, Ayurveda, our old "science of longevity"; and that too pronounced the death sentence upon me. But instead of waiting for death to take me, the priest left me in the charge of a Brahmachari, a young monk, and hunted for a Hathayogi. Now you know Hathayogis are a fraternity of semi-holy men who heal and do other tricks. Most of them can perform miracles.

About an hour before midnight, according to those who were present, Purohit brought a Hathayogi. The Gods alone know how he found the man.

The only thing that I can vividly recall was three men's faces bending over me. I looked at them for a moment in spite of the keen pain that was cutting into my body, and instead of passing into another spell of delirium my gaze was fastened upon those faces. One of them looked at me. He was speaking: "It is not, it is not, it is not." Now he lifted one hand from under his tunic and put it on my head. It was so cool. It almost cleared my head; like a drop of ice cold water that coolness slid to my spine, then down, down toward my feet, and like layers of steaming woollen coverlets, the oppressive heat that had been smothering me slowly lifted—one coverlet at a time. And with it began the easing of the excruciating agony of my body. I felt so exhausted that I fell asleep instantly.

I am told that I slept a day and a half steadily, but at last when I did awake, I was a healed man.*

I was confined to my bed, however, for a fortnight longer. It was nearly a month before I could take a long walk. During that time I saw the wizard that healed me twice more.

* As a substantiation of the above, even in as recent a time as 1920–1921, a Hathayogi named Dheap Narain performed some cures in the city of Allahabad. He had the reputation of healing people even from the bites of cobras. His work was quite inexplicable.

After his first visit he kept away a few days, then since I seemed always to suffer from a degree of unrelenting fever Purohit, who had been nursing me, grew frightened again. He kept on grumbling: "This fever bothers me. If you are healed, why does not the miserable fever depart altogether? I have a great mind to run after that wizard once more!"

Surprising though it may sound the fellow had apparently heard the priest's thought, for lo, within several days, he reappeared. I saw him now, not with eyes half-stricken with delirium, but with a clear mind which perceived in him something very hard. He was bare to the waist, the rest of him was wrapped in a loin-cloth of ochre which indicated that he was a Sannyasina, a mendicant monk. Though he had his uniform, so to speak, I doubted if he was totally consecrated to holiness. His face had a lean look, and his eyes were like small searchlights. The man lacked the supreme mark of holiness—detachment.

As he squatted on the floor near my chanpie, or cot, I thanked him profusely, but this seemed to irritate him, and he said sharply: "Why do you thank me, boy; I but acquired merit!"

Just as I was about to answer he shot at me a strange question: "Why are you still grieving for that aunt of yours?"

I replied: "My Lord, I cannot help it."

The teacher smacked his lips. "You should not grieve, for she is not dead. Her body is burnt up. I see her soul standing behind you, my child. She is telling me to tell you not to grieve. How does she look? Ha, you young sceptic! You think I do not really see her—I will tell you." Then he gave an exact description of my aunt. He even told me how her big toe always stood apart from her other toes when she stood.

"How do you know all this?" said the priest.

"Because this boy's sorrowing is holding his aunt's soul to earth. She goes with him wherever he goes. Through long practise of religious austerity and many penances, I have pleased God. He gave me the boon of reading thoughts and seeing into a man's heart. I use my powers to help people. I want to help you, boy. How can I do so if you make yourself sick by grieving? Don't grieve! If you do you will keep your aunt's soul here. Give her freedom! Rejoice, that she may resume her Godward journey, for she was old, and she had served you long; release her from serving you any further!"

"Must I forget her, my Lord?" I asked in anguish.

"No. Keep her memory alive, but don't depend upon her. Be strong. Help *her!*"

That sounded very sensible to me, young though I was. She, who had poured into me so much strength and wisdom must not find me weak. I owed her at least that much. I must not hold her down. "I must be strong, I must be strong," I repeated to my secret self.

As if he had read my thought the fellow said: "Strength begets strength. God loves the strong. He has not much love for the weak." With these words he asked for a glass of water. Forthwith the priest brought it. I was asked to hold it in my hand. In a few moments the wizard touched the outside of the glass with his finger. Instantly the water within the glass began to boil and bubble. He removed his hand for a moment; the contents of the glass became calm. Again he touched it, and at once the water began to dance.

After the second time he said to me: "If you drink this water, it will make you strong. Drink it, little soul of power."

I did as I was bid. Then he rose to leave, saying: "You are to lead a life of adventure and power. Be strong. Make your soul fit for such a life. You are healed. Farewell."

In a few seconds we heard the clatter of his slippers outside on the stone courtyard of our serai, or inn. Within a week I was able to take a walk. I grew eager to return to Mayavati, but the priest insisted on keeping me in Benares a few more days.

"Though outwardly Benares is commercial," he gave his elaborated reason, "at heart it is a very spiritual city. There is no older city. Here the Incarnation of God, Buddha Deva (Lord Buddha) preached and lived. Here Krishna propounded our Bible, the Gita. In Benares you will find not only the best of the past, but also of India's present. Let us seek for a holy man and ask him for wisdom."

Of course, I obeyed Purohit, who had been a father to me, and we visited all manner of religious teachers, most of whom were not quite holy. More than a dozen so-called teachers taught, not because they had seen God, but because they made a living by it. To them religion was a means of livelihood. This, I suppose, is true of the great bulk of the preachers all over the world.

I also looked for our wizard who was not to be found in his usual haunts. Our reason for searching for him was to give him a little present as a symbol of my appreciation of his kindness. I felt that though he had acquired merit by saving my life, I must express my gratitude by giving him a purse containing several gold coins.

At last by sheer chance we located him on a step of the Dasashwamedha Ghaut one morning. He was reading aloud from a Sanskrit book, though thousands of pilgrims, men, women and children, walked up and down the vast steps near him, clamouring and shouting. As soon as we sat down by him he stopped reading.

I noticed that he seemed pleased to see us again. "Ha, what keeps you in Benares? Are you not well? Do you want another drink of magic water?"

"No, sir," I answered humbly, "I wish to express my gratitude to you." I gave him the little purse. He took it, and said with a laugh: "I am glad I am not altogether holy, for then I would have a lot of disciples who would take all my earnings, as farmers rob their milch cows."

"Are you not completely?" asked Purohit.

"Friend, I am no spiritual teacher. I am a little better than a common magician. No, I have not seen God. I have some occult powers," the wizard continued. "If I were a completely religious man, I would not do any tricks or miracles. A truly religious teacher never does tricks, never!" Then changing the subject he said: "I see into your future. Next year I see you in queer company. You are going to seek out a man who carries cats in a cage. He is a performer. The coming winter he will teach you about taming animals, but you must grow very very strong! Even now you have not given up sorrowing altogether."

With these words the strange man dismissed us. Was I content? I must say that I was. That day and many times later I said to myself: "Be strong. Be strong!" No doubt this did lift up my soul from sorrow, and what is more, I believe that mourning for the dead is not good for the souls that have left their bodies. Our old Hindu ideal of Shraddha—rejoicing with love—for the last rites, is very sound; that alone can help the departed souls to reach the end of their Godward path. Shraddha is the right form of funeral.*

Now that the month of mourning enjoined by religion was over, we decided to go to Mayavati to perform Shraddha. But before we left Benares by a strange piece of good fortune we encountered a true holy man. We found him one day in Durga Bari—the Temple of the Mother of the Universe. The place is so infested with monkeys that sometimes it is called by fools "The Monkey Temple." But you see, the Deity being the Mother of the Uni-

* Shraddha is a feast of rejoicing given by the community after death to augment the soul's power of flight. One month is allowed for mourning and then the ceremony of Shraddha is performed to help free the soul from the fetters of Grief.

verse does not say "No" even to monkeys and cows. All are welcome to Her house.

It was on a quiet morning when all the worshippers had left, that we found a man seated there against a sculptured pillar of the pavilion in front of the inner shrine. He had been looking at the people that came and went and appeared like a sculptor watching such movements of men as would be desirable to carve in stone. He was not at all aware at first that we were looking at him, but at last when he did so, showed no embarrassment, but signed to us to come and sit near him. His oval face, high forehead, square jaw and almost white complexion betokened something unusual. "Benares is the only city that never ceases to interest one!" he said to us.

We agreed with him.

"Three thousand years have been made immortal by temples only, without mention of builder or donor. There is no personal record of any kind in Benares; no mausoleum, no palaces, no pictures, no theatres—nothing personal has been created to commemorate any event—always temples to God or to the Gods, century after century, they erected here. No wonder that even the bulls that wander idly through these streets look as benevolent as saints; cows and saints are our best citizens here!"

"But so many cows, and hardly one saint," complained Purohit.

"Yes," rejoined the holy man. "But if saints were as numerous as cows and monkeys, where would you house them?"

"Are they so hard to accommodate?" the priest inquired.

"They are," he answered. "A saint is he who lives with God. Such an one is generally harsh to the priests and pompous worshippers who flatter themselves by performing rituals, by practising charity and by taking the name of God. A saint's scorn withers them. It is better that we rarely have a saint. He makes most people very uncomfortable."

"Have you seen God?" I asked suddenly and without knowing why I did so, just as I might have asked casually and irrelevantly, for his address.

He looked at me calmly for a while without the tremor of an eyelash, and as a person speaking from the profoundest conviction, he said: "Yes!" Then in order to hide the fire that had come into his eyes he closed them. If a tiger had leaped into our midst the effect could not have been so startling as that simple and clear "Yes."

Purohit, a Brahmin of Brahmins, the highest caste in the world, bent down his head and took the dust from that man's feet. There was no doubt that he was holy.

After saluting him thus humbly we arose in silence to go. The holy one said: "Peace goes with you." As if it were true, the priest and I departed without a word. We packed our belongings and started for Mayavati. It will surprise you to know that during our entire journey we hardly spoke to one another. I dared not for I was afraid that every word would dissipate the peace that had come into my soul, and in the silence I heard all the more

eloquently the peace that dwelt also in the soul of Purohit. All important religious truths have been communicated from man to man through silence.

At Mayavati, after our arrival, we held a great feast of rejoicing. We fed the poor and gave away many presents. One full day we spent in such religious rites as augmented my aunt's Godward journey. Instead of pain, only peace dwelt in our home. Throughout the rites of Shraddha, one sentiment was repeated again and again:

> "Rejoice, O soul, in thy new Home!
> Put on thy vesture of effulgence, since
> You dwell now where all longings are fulfilled!"

XIX—End of Adolescence

I DID not meet the circus performer with his cats in a cage the following winter as the wizard had prophesied, but two years later. That shows the uncertainty of prophecies. Now in my old age I believe that if you are credulous enough, you will adhere to all the prophecies about yourself whether they fulfill themselves or not. The art of the wizard or a prophet is soundly based, for it is founded on man's chronic malady of hoping. He who hopes the most swallows any amount of prophecy.

Now I must tell you how I spent the following winter. After I had settled down to the task of being the head of our household in Mayavati since Kuri was gone, the priest advised me to tame more animals. He offered to help me in my undertaking, and the reason he gave me for resuming my pleasure in animals was because the panther Mita's treachery had made me suspicious of cats, and of the animal world in general. And I must conquer that sense of suspicion ere it became firmly rooted in my soul.

Sar, the dog, was still with me; so also were the pigeons. I had to buy a baby cheeta for I could procure no panther nor leopard cub. Cheetas, as you know, are very much like leopards save that their claws are different from a cat's. They cannot climb trees, nor do the strokes of their forefeet kill at once a deer or a nilgai, a blue deer. It is the momentum of their leap and their bite that they depend upon to finish their prey. Cheetas may be trained to hunt and to bring their kill to their trainers in the same fashion as the trained shikra, falcon, brings his victim as an offering to the falconer, but of all that I shall speak in its proper time and place.

I wish to tell you now of a surprise visit from a lost friend of mine which brought me joy and made my lonesome home happier. It was the sudden return from the woods of Benji, the mongoose. One dry clear day, about the end of autumn, three members of a mongoose family came and nosed about the outer entrance of my home. I, who was on the roof watching my pigeons sunning themselves, was interested in the three black quadrupeds. They withdrew from the door and hid themselves behind a large haycock just a few yards away from the house, then they reappeared and vanished again, but not for long. The smallest one looked like my own Benji, but Benji, I thought, could not be so small now. He must have grown quite large—then who were these three people?

As if their conferences were over, one of the two larger animals took leave of his companions who waited near the haycock, but instead of going away he came to our entrance door and entered the house. After a moment more he climbed to the roof where I was looking after the pigeons. Though the latter had forgotten him, he felt a shock of joy at seeing them, for it was indeed Benji! At close range it did not take me a minute to identify him. He too knew me at once. Not only Benji, but every Mongoose I have ever known, shows a tremendously retentive memory. It was thrilling to watch him respond to my recognition of him. At first his whole body, now grown quite large, quivered, then his little whiskers stiffened, and as I took him up in my hand his hair stood on end. We looked at each other as might two camels lost in a desert when they find one another near a water-hole after days of thirst and wandering on the scorching sands.

After a few moments he jumped off my hand and ran to his family. I surmised that the two waiting outside were his wife and child. He had a long conference with them. I could quite follow their argument; though he pressed them to come to me they declined to do so for the time being, so he returned with his family to the woods whence they had come. After they had gone, I wondered how that pair of mongoose came to breed. You do know this—but a mongoose who is tamed and attached to man rarely breeds. I have never heard of any pair having children if one or both of them were in human company. The very fact of living with man, no matter how freely, prevents them from breeding. That is the law of mongoose life. Because I knew this, and because Benji's family had proven itself an exception to the rule, I felt deeply touched by his return to me with his wife and child.

But that return did not take place at once. After the first day's short visit, he and his family came day after day for half an hour at a time. Benji came to me, but the others stayed as far away as the entrance to our house. Since they never made their call at any appointed time, I had to wait for them, which was good for me, keeping my mind interested and alert, and off other things. I would go about looking for all kinds of sweet food for them, which took a good deal of time, and when they did come, generally some time in the afternoon, I was happy to serve them with what I had secured. Thus in the course of a couple of months I won the confidence of all three of them and soon they made their home with me.

With the coming of winter the priest and I began to go out in order to spend some hours in the jungle. If we went in the daytime I took the dog, Sar, and the entire mongoose family, but if it was night I took the mongoose alone. They rarely objected to my doing so.

What a winter's night can be in the jungle is indicated by the absence of mosquitoes and many vile insects. Even the serpents were sleeping in their holes. There was nothing to be troubled by on a tree top, and plenty to observe below owing to the falling off of most of the leaves from the trees and saplings. You could find many more beasts exposed to your view at this time of the year than usual.

One night, the last week of February, seeing that spring was near, we took all three of the mongoose to the jungle. Our aim was to leave them to their own devices until the end of summer when they would return home. It was not good for them to be even remotely connected with man now that the time for breeding was approaching.

Well, it was fortunate that we took them with us. Had we not done so, I at least would not be here to tell the tale.

It was a magnificent night, not quite so cold as heretofore. Already the sap was running so vigorously in the trees that one could almost hear it. Buds and berries were already putting forth coy fingers to the touch of the wind. The spring was shy that year. She put forth a hand today and withdrew it the next. What hesitancy, what enchantment!

That night about eight o'clock we made ourselves at home on the limb of an unusually large nut tree on which we had erected a machan, or seat. The three mongoose sat on our laps; the priest held two, and I kept Benji. I was on the outerside, while between me and the trunk was Purohit. He was getting old, and since he wished to sleep he preferred to have his back against the trunk.

Instead of being still as was their wont, that night the mongoose family was restless. Each one of them was so agitated that the priest inferred their malady to be spring fever. But malady or no malady, their restlessness made both of us human beings nervous. The priest grumbled and complained that he could not sleep, and I grew agitated because he talked and they fretted. That there was peril hemming us in we could not doubt, but since there was nothing to be done about it we stayed where we were. There was nowhere to go at half past ten when the moon was rising and setting astir not only boars and buffaloes, but also the tigers who were prowling all about.

Under our tree passed an elephant, the first one to come north. He vanished like a black barge into a silvered darkness. Well, if the Hathi were coming north in February that meant spring had begun at least ten days earlier than usual, his heat-loving skin does not like the lower Himalayas except when the warmth is guaranteed. His presence told us that we must be careful, for migrating animals are generally hungry and ill-tempered. They kill out of sheer temper.

But on a tree top we felt quite safe. About the middle of the night a small herd of Hathis passed. Following them came not stray buffaloes, the usual winter inhabitants of the jungle, but immigrating herds. One of them came very near us, but the rest passed far away from where we were. Only the moo-ings of their chiefs told us that they had had scent of a tiger or leopard.

Soon that was over, and the jungle became still. Everything was so calm that if one of the three animals moved on our laps it made a stir in the whole air.

But they kept on moving. I put my hand on Benji's back. It hurt me; for his hair was standing on end, stiff as barbs. In that deep shadow cast by the upper boughs where we sat, nothing could be seen by my poor human eyes, so I was forced to listen. There was hardly the flicker of a sound at first, as if heavy doors of stillness had locked us in.

On a sudden Benji sat up, then crouched on my lap. Now a sharp point of noise, I could perceive, began to scratch on the fast locked gate of stillness. It rose higher. Passing from a scratch, it mounted some unknown scales and struck a new note—that of an end of a lash making designs on the grass that complained. It drew nearer and grew louder. "F—s—sh" it scolded. Benji coughed and leaped off my lap. "F—ss—sh—bang," then a terrific explosion of crackling dry leaves below on the ground. The priest shouted to me that his charges, the son and wife of Benji, had joined the fray, and as I stood up to go down, he held my legs with one hand. He would not let me go. "What good can you do in that blinding dark place? Let the three mongoose fight one viper. Sit still until day breaks. O God, what a night!"

The priest had aged rapidly this one year. Since he had no love of adventure and because he sat between me and the tree-trunk, I could not walk over him, and so I obeyed him.

In the morning when we descended we found only a cobra's head lying on the ground. The three little animals that had saved my life were playing hide and seek after their sumptuous breakfast.

It was the biggest cobra's head I had even seen, nearly as large as my palm. Imagine its size when he was alive and spreading his hood. After examining the entire ground, we found how he had come there. He must have thrown off his skin after his winter's sleep, and in his new skin he was very handsome. He felt hungry as all serpents do after nearly three to four months' hibernation; he must have seen some birds going northward, and towards nightfall he went up our tree and found on the farthest end of the bough where our platform was a small duck, a straggler, resting for the night. So as soon as it grew dark enough he caught the poor fellow and set to swallow it. And after his dinner was over he went to sleep. When he awoke he found that between him and the trunk of the tree were human beings and at least one mongoose.

Suppose now that night we had not taken Benji and his family with us. What would have happened? We do not need to pursue that idea now. How clear and quick Benji's leap was and how certain his bite we could surmise by the head of the snake which had been cut off just where, were it a human head, its Adam's apple would be. Think of doing such a neat job in the dark!

After this victory over death we felt too sentimental to abandon my mongoose trio in the jungle that day, so we brought them home to proclaim to our community how well we had been served by our three friends. The distended belly of each mongoose corroborated our evidence with the most vivid eloquence.

That was my last adventure in the jungle for the time being. For some years to come my experience of animals was confined to taming and playing with them in a circus. Of that in the next instalment. In the meantime let me stop here, O friend and pupil of my heart. May the Gods keep you from hurt and harm! May felicity abide with you for ever, and may you compel victory in every undertaking of life. For the time being permit me, O Diadem of wisdom, and the Soul of enjoyment to say

TAMAM